ANTONIN ARTAUD
From Theory to Practice

Lee Jamieson

GREENWICH EXCHANGE
LONDON

Greenwich Exchange, London

Antonin Artaud
From Theory to Practice

© Lee Jamieson, 2007

First published in Great Britain in 2007
Reprinted 2010

Printed and bound by imprintdigital.net
Typesetting and design by Albion Associates
Cover design by December Publications
Tel: 028 90286559
Cover image: Jack Thurgar

Greenwich Exchange Website: www.greenex.co.uk

Cataloguing in Publication Data is available
from the British Library

ISBN: 978-1-871551-98-3

Dedicated to the health of Vicki Jamieson

Thanks to Justyn Tandy

Contents

Chronology

Note: Due to the highly fractured nature of Artaud's work, made up of letters, individually published essays, reviews and public lectures, this chronology has a bias towards his theatre related activities.

1896   Born on 4th September in Marseilles, France to Euphrasie (née Nalpas) and Antoine-Roi Artaud. The eldest of three children. Premiere of Alfred Jarry's controversial *Ubu Roi* in Paris.

1901   Contracts meningitis triggering a series of nervous disorders during his life.

1910   Begins writing his first poems and publishes a literary magazine at school. His grandmother dies.

1914-15   Outbreak of First World War. Suffers from his first bout of depression during which he destroys all of his early writing. His parents organise a short stay in a sanatorium.

1916   Manages to publish some early poetry. Serves for less than a year in the military. Discharged for medical reasons.

1917-18   His mental and physical health problems persist, resulting in a number of sanatorium stays, the longest in Switzerland, where he is prescribed opium for the first time. End of First World War resulting in revolution in Germany.

1920	Moves to Paris and lodges with the psychologist Edouard Toulouse. Contributes to Toulouse's literary activities including editing a collection of his essays and contributing to his journal, *Demain*.
1921	Begins working in the theatre. Trains with Charles Dullin and joins his experimental theatre in Montmartre – the Atelier Theatre.
1922	His essay and poetry writing gains momentum alongside his theatre-acting career. During a return trip to Marseilles, he sees a performance by a troupe of Cambodian dancers, an event that informs his growing theatre theory.
1923	Jacques Rivière, the editor of *La Nouvelle Revue Française*, rejects his poems, but they begin corresponding.
1924	Publishes his first important theatre essay, 'The Evolution of Set Design'. His 'Correspondence with Jacques Rivière' continues until June and is published in the September edition of *La Nouvelle Revue Française*. His father dies a few days later. Joins the Surrealist Party in October.
1925	Acts in Abel Gance's film *Napoléon*. Edits the third edition of the Surrealist Party's newspaper, *La Révolution Surréaliste*. Publishes two short books entitled *Umbilical Limbo* and *Nerve Scales*. Collected in *Umbilical Limbo* is the play *The Spurt of Blood*.
1926	Forms the short-lived Theatre of Alfred Jarry and publishes a manifesto for the project. André Breton expels Artaud from the Surrealist Party because he was resisting the new political direction of the movement.
1927	The Theatre of Alfred Jarry continues throughout the year. Writes a film scenario entitled *The Seashell and*

the Clergyman which is directed by Germaine Dulac between July and September. Artaud is unavailable for filming because he is acting in Carl Theodor Dreyer's *The Passion of Joan of Arc*.

1928   *The Passion of Joan of Arc* and *The Seashell and the Clergyman* are both released, but Artaud is furious about the changes made by Dulac to his original scenario. After a few chaotic performances, the Theatre of Alfred Jarry crumbles.

1929   Writes *The Philosopher's Stone*. Publishes *Art and Death*.

1931   Sends *The Philosopher's Stone* to Louis Jouvet for his consideration. Jouvet does not commission the project. Sees a troupe of Balinese dancers perform at the colonial exposition in Paris. He publishes a review of the performance, later to be incorporated into *The Theatre and its Double*. Forms the concept of a Theatre of Cruelty. Delivers 'Production and Metaphysics' at the Sorbonne (included in *The Theatre and its Double*).

1932   His first manifesto for the Theatre of Cruelty is published in *La Nouvelle Revue Française*, now edited by Jean Paulhan, who offers Artaud his creative and financial support. In later life, Artaud claimed to have met Hitler in a cafe during a trip to Berlin, Germany.

1933   Delivers 'Theatre and the Plague' at the Sorbonne, which is later collected in *The Theatre and its Double*. Burning of the Reichstag. Hitler takes power in Germany.

1934   In an attempt to raise funds for the Theatre of Cruelty, Artaud gives a public reading of *The Conquest of Mexico*. Begins working on a script for *The Cenci*.

1935   *The Cenci* goes into production, but financially collapses after only 17 performances. Humiliated, Artaud plans to leave for Mexico. Proposes collecting his many essays and manifestos into book form.

1936   Travels to Mexico where he lectures at the university and joins the Tarahumara Indians to witness their peyote ritual. His month-long experience with the Tarahumara has a deep and lasting impact. Towards the end of the year he returns to Paris.

1937   His mental health deteriorates. After acquiring a walking stick that he believed originally belonged to Saint Patrick, Artaud travels to Ireland. The journey is disastrous and he is deported in a straightjacket. Upon arrival in France, he is interned until 1946.

1938   Although living in an asylum in Paris, *The Theatre and its Double* is published as planned.

1939   Outbreak of Second World War.

1940   Fall of Paris to the Nazis and introduction of starvation rations. As a mental patient in the occupied zone, Artaud suffers from malnutrition.

1943   Artaud is transferred away from Paris to an asylum in Rodez, outside the Nazi occupied zone. Although he is better cared for, his new doctor, Gaston Ferdière, subjects Artaud to electroshock therapy.

1944   Second edition of *The Theatre and its Double* is published. Paris liberated from Nazi control.

1945   Second World War ends.

1946   Released from Rodez, Artaud returns to a liberated Paris where he is allowed to live in his own accommodation within the grounds of an asylum. He is given a key to the gate and is allowed free movement. An auction of artworks donated by famous French writers and artists ensures Artaud's financial future. He signs a publishing contract for his *Collected Works*.

1947   Makes his final public appearance at the Vieux-Colombier Theatre in Paris, where he lectures on his life's artistic activities. The event is met with mixed reviews. Begins writing and rehearsing a radio production entitled *To Have Done with the Judgement of God*.

1948   Receives the Sainte-Beuve award for his essay 'Van Gogh: The Man Suicided by Society'. His radio production is banned one day preceding broadcast. He is diagnosed with an inoperable cancer shortly after. He entrusts the editing of his *Collected Works* to Paule Thévenin. Artaud dies alone on 4th March.

Introduction

On 13th January 1947, Antonin Artaud made his final public appearance on the small stage of the Vieux-Colombier Theatre in Paris. Promoted as *A Tête-à-tête with Antonin Artaud*, the event was eagerly anticipated by the literary and artistic elite of post-war France. All 900 seats were filled and more than half again were turned away at the door.

The now notorious event started as planned with the reading of three poems. Commanding the full attention of his audience, Artaud began speaking but started to loose coherency. He nervously mumbled and spluttered his way through the texts, hesitating and leaving elongated silences. Finally, he came to a standstill and, unable to continue, broke for an interval. The second half of Artaud's lecture-cum-performance is now infamous. He began reading but dropped his manuscript. As his papers spilled across the stage, Artaud stood motionless and in silence. Suddenly, he broke out into a fierce torrent of improvised screams and convulsions, incandescently attacking the causes of his life's suffering and claiming that dark forces were stalking him. He sustained this vehement bombardment for two hours until midnight, when he eventually came to a stop. In the silence that followed, Artaud looked out at the sea of bewildered expressions and finally turned upon his audience. Reportedly, he accused the spectators of being disinterested in his opinions and promptly stormed off stage, never again to make another public appearance.

The accounts of that night in January vary enormously. Some saw the breakdown of a mentally-ill man, others saw a momentous failure, whilst a select group perceived a genius demolishing the acceptable boundaries of theatre. However, a common denominator can be found in each of the contrasting reports. Artaud himself identified this in a letter written shortly after the event where he maintained that the 'performance' was more real and emotional than any fictional play could ever be. Either intentionally or unintentionally, Artaud presented himself as the 'subject' of the performance.

In some respects, all of Artaud's work has been blighted by failure – his productions never matched the brilliance of his theories, publishers rejected his poetry and his public appearances were more sensational than successful. It therefore seems fitting that, in his last public appearance, Artaud presented himself as a defeated madman on the brink of collapse.

The failure and rejection that surrounded his writing seems a strange precursor for his undeniable influence over contemporary theatre. Today, the ideas and terms invented by Artaud have become a vital part of theatre's everyday vocabulary. Reviews brand inventive productions with the 'Artaudian' mark, critics analyse performance with reference to his theories and practitioners use the Theatre of Cruelty as a framework upon which to build their own ideas. Yet a concrete definition of Artaud's theatre is problematic to formulate and the case 'against' him is persuasive. It is all too simple to suggest that Artaud failed, a conclusion easily reached if we assume that Artaud's aesthetic project terminated on the day he deceased. However, a writer's work remains active long after their death, and therefore, a study of Artaud's theory and practice per se is insufficient. To fully estimate the importance of Artaud's writing, we must also investigate why the questions he asked are still reverberating in today's contemporary culture. This approach has informed the writing of this book.

The key to understanding the relationship between Artaud's theory and practice is to identify the central belief that operates from the core of his writing. As we shall discover, Artaud is a doctrinaire who casts his net wider than the discipline of theatre. For him, theatre was simply a suitable vehicle for his socio-philosophical beliefs, of which his theatre proposals were a by-product. Furthermore, Artaud's own relationship with theatre was inconstant, frequently questioning its ability to realise his philosophical stance. Perhaps the events that occurred during his final public appearance were a repercussion of his disillusionment with theatre. His discontent is evident in a letter written two weeks after the event to the surrealist poet André Breton:

> I left because I realized that the only language I could use on an audience was to take bombs out of my pockets and throw them in their faces in a gesture of unmistakable aggression.
>
> (*Artaud on Theatre*, p.205)

Although I locate Artaud's theatre philosophically and culturally in Chapter 3, 'The Disease of the West', these ideas thread throughout the other chapters as they do in Artaud's own writing. This book follows these ideas from theory to practice, examining Artaud's contribution to performance and assessing the extent to which he compromised his vision. The final chapter explores his posthumous influence over theatre and reviews contemporary responses to his ideas. What this book reveals is that, many years after his death, Artaud's work remains fresh, contemporary and as potent as ever. In his own lifetime, he was significant only to the French literary and artistic scene, yet a decade later, he was given iconic status by the 1960s counter-culture.

Today, contemporary theatre is indebted to Artaud. The questions he asked persist in shaking conventional theatre to its very core and continue to unlock new approaches to performance. His influence is broad – writers such as Jean Genet and Samuel Beckett, directors such as Peter Brook and Jerzy Grotowski, companies such as Théâtre de Complicité and the Living Theatre, genres such as physical theatre and performance art, choreographers such as Pina Bausch and Merce Cunningham – all of these owe a debt to Antonin Artaud.

Artaud's presence has already eclipsed 20th-century theatre and his ideas have become inseparable from it. Consequently, his influence will continue to exert itself and inform fresh 21st-century perspectives.

Today, his fingerprints are everywhere and he overshadows the architecture of modern theatre.

Even now, he remains our contemporary.

1

Art and Madness

Even though Antonin Artaud left behind over 20 volumes of his *Collected Works*, he remains an enigma. Because his artistic achievements crossed the boundaries of any single discipline, it is impossible to pigeonhole his work. He was equally regarded as an influential poet, theatre director, theorist, actor, visual artist and film practitioner, yet it is impossible to examine one without discussing the other. Rather than confining his work to a single area, Artaud considered himself a 'creative force' strong enough to sweep away the boundaries that distinguish one discipline from another. This concept of radical change is the driving force behind all of Artaud's writing. He proposed the abolition of conventional theatre, redesigning it as a place capable of 'confronting' people rather than 'entertaining' them. However, Artaud's moments of brilliance were interrupted by periods of illness, drug addiction, poverty and sanatorium stays. Consequently, his writing and his theatre productions seem inconsistent. His influential book of collected essays, entitled *The Theatre and its Double,* develops no clear guidelines on how to put his theatre into practice. Instead, it offers little more than a series of radical images and concepts that contemporary theatre makers have deciphered in their own way. It is for this reason that Artaud's work is notoriously difficult to read and why many commentators have found it impossible to separate his life from his writing. As the critic Alan Read observed, "there is a sense in which it has been Artaud's life, rather than *The Theatre and Its Double*, which presents us with the significant text to be examined for the theatre. It is in itself an extended performance." It is this premise that informs our point of departure – a short biography with which to frame our reading of Artaud's work. Consequently, many of the ideas, theories and concepts explored in this book will be traced back to the following account of Artaud's colourful, yet tragic life.

Walking the fine line between art and madness

Antonin Artaud was born in the southern French city of Marseilles on 4th September 1896 into a devoutly religious family. Although in later life Artaud widely condemned Christianity, his religious upbringing echoes throughout his theories, poems and plays. Most notably, he discussed his proposed theatre in 'spiritual' terms, claiming that it should be a kind of 'communion' between audience and performer. Significantly, Artaud's lifelong health problems started at an early age, suffering from neuralgia, a condition that causes pain in the nerves, and a life-threatening attack of meningitis at the age of four. By 17 he was disruptive, suffering from depression and consequently failing at school. Concerned for the mental health of their son, Artaud's parents had him admitted into a series of sanatoriums over the next five years where he was first prescribed opium for his mental health problems, triggering his lifelong addiction to narcotics. Throughout his life, Artaud underwent many detoxification treatments to try to rid himself of his addiction but always succumbed to his cravings. Images of his addiction reoccur throughout his work, sometimes explicitly. Notably, Artaud published a text entitled 'Letter to the Legislator of the Drug Act' (included in his first book, *Umbilical Limbo*) in which he railed against the state legislation that had made it difficult and expensive for him to medicate against his pain. He distinguishes between two types of drug addicts, those that are "kick-seeking" and those that are "sick". He argued that it was only those who genuinely needed opium to relieve their physical and mental anguish that obtained their supplies from pharmacies, the rest had always acquired it through illegal means. Therefore, 'legitimate' drug addicts had been abandoned by the state and their right to control their pain had been placed in the hands of gangsters. The text also reveals the devastating effect of Artaud's ill health upon his life; without the drugs, he is overcome by an all-encompassing anguish from which he cannot escape. His suffering informed the tone of his writing, viscerally conveying the pain of both his mind and body.

Although still in care, Artaud decided to move north to Paris and become a writer and actor. Horrified, his parents tried to dissuade him from such a venture, but Artaud insisted, eventually agreeing to be transferred into the care of a Parisian doctor investigating artistic genius. Plans were made and, at the age of 23, Artaud eagerly set off for a new life in Paris, lodging in the home of his new doctor for the first six months. Following that, Artaud's living arrangements became increasingly erratic, moving between friends' homes, hostels and cheap hotels. He scrapped by as a theatre actor, learning his craft over a four-year period, moving from production to production. However, Artaud's erratic performance technique made it increasingly more difficult for him to secure roles. Finally, he managed to break into film acting, albeit with the help of his film producer cousin, Louis Nalpas, an aspect of his artistic career that lasted for ten years. In fact, Artaud was moderately successful as a film actor, taking over 20 roles between 1924 and 1935 and performing in two of France's most significant silent films of the 1920s: *The Passion of Joan of Arc* and *Napoléon*. Although Artaud occasionally felt compromised by the commercialisation of the film industry, it did help him to fund his more avant-garde theatre projects.

During this period, Artaud's poetry and prose were becoming increasingly more fragmented. His poetry describes the anguish he feels when he is forced to use conventional words to convey his inner thoughts. Deep down, Artaud feels ideas stir inside him, but cannot express them through language. In translating these primal ideas into written text, the crux of the original thought, idea or emotion is lost because conventional words are incapable of conveying such experiences. Artaud's dilemma is that to express himself, he must write, yet writing cannot express what he wants to say. He notes that:

> Once spoken, all speech is dead and is only active as it is spoken. Once a form is used it has no more use, bidding man find another form …
>
> (*Collected Works*: *Volume 4*, p.75)

From his arrival in Paris, Artaud wanted to be accepted by the literary and artistic scene of the time. This required the most important literary journal in Paris, *La Nouvelle Revue Française*, publishing his work. Artaud approached the editor, Jacques Rivière, with examples of his work, but Rivière decided that the submission was unprintable because it was too far removed from the standard conventions of poetry. However, he offered to meet the young writer and discuss his work with him. A correspondence was initiated in which Artaud's poetic struggle to find a language capable of expressing his inner thoughts was debated, and ironically it was this series of letters that was published in the journal rather than the poetry itself. (The content of these letters and Artaud's attitude towards language will be dealt with in more detail in Chapter 3.) It was this event that sparked Artaud's literary career and identified him as a growing talent in the Parisian arts scene.

Artaud's published 'Correspondence with Jacques Rivière' attracted the interest of André Breton who was leading the emerging Surrealist Party in 1920s Paris. The surrealists were exploring the potential of using the subconscious and dream imagery to develop new forms of artistic presentation. For example, surrealist poets like Paul Eluard would randomly join unrelated objects and concepts to create dream effects, whilst artists like Salvador Dali and René Magritte attempted to paint dreamscapes, placing everyday objects in incongruous contexts. The ultimate aim of the surrealist movement was to unleash the 'inner' self and free human desire from the consciousness. Thus, Artaud's struggle to find a poetic form of expression capable of communicating his inner thought strongly appealed to the surrealist project. The surrealist movement became an ideal platform for Artaud's work, not only because it provided a readership for his writing, but also because it brought him into contact with artists who understood the anguish he experienced when writing. By 1925, Artaud had become an important figure in the party, had been nominated director of The Surrealist Research Centre and had been given complete editorial control over the society's third edition of their newspaper, *La Révolution Surréaliste.* In this issue, Artaud attacked all aspects of Western civilisation through a series of open letters to university chancellors, the Pope, the Dalai Lama, the Buddhist schools and directors of lunatic asylums.[1] 'Letter to the Chancellors of the European Universities' accuses academia of imposing a false logic upon the world that is incapable of revealing the complexities of the mind or the emotions of the heart. Believing that the prophets of the past were more in touch with the universe, Artaud called for an end to the factory-like model of education where students are 'milled' through their diplomas. In 'Address to the Pope', Artaud endeavoured to completely deflate the authority of Catholicism and its leader, claiming that God does not speak through the Pope, that the priests serving God's will are corrupt, and that the doctrine upheld by the church is a fallacy. The spiritual decline of the West is remedied in 'Letter to the Dalai Lama' and 'Letter to the Buddhist Schools' in which Artaud idealises their belief systems. He asks the Dalai Lama to 'decontaminate' Western civilisation of its problems and show the European people how to escape the controlling influence of the Pope and academia. This was to be achieved by following Buddhist beliefs which reflect the wholeness of life, whereas the Western disposition divides and rationalises human experience.

Artaud's involvement with the surrealists came to an abrupt end when, in 1926, Breton had him expelled from the party. Breton wanted the party to embrace Marxist ideology and campaign for a political revolution in France. Artaud disagreed and set up his first theatre company with some allies from the Surrealist Party. The company's title, the Theatre of Alfred Jarry, was homage to the outrageous French playwright of the same name, whose infamous play, *Ubu Roi,* premiered the year Artaud was born. Notoriously, this was the first play on the French stage to include the word 'Shit'! It took 15 riotous minutes for the audience to get over their astonishment and it was probably this disruption in the auditorium that appealed to Artaud. *Ubu Roi* was heralded as the forerunner to the surrealist movement, and as such, Artaud was making reference to the surrealist essence of his new theatre work by using Jarry's name. Although Artaud refused to publicly admit any connection with the Surrealist Party from which he had been expelled, his new theatre was clearly influenced by the movement, aiming to stage impossible dreamscapes and chaotic hallucinations which were akin to the surrealist's interest in the subconscious.

The Theatre of Alfred Jarry lasted only two seasons, Artaud's financial situation deteriorated, his drug addiction worsened and he was now isolated from the artistic scene in Paris of which he had tried so hard to be a part. Although his experiences with surrealism and theatre had both ended in failure, they provided the essential building blocks for the development of his most ambitious project, the Theatre of Cruelty.

The Theatre of Cruelty

Between 1931 and 1935, Artaud developed one of theatre history's most influential concepts – the Theatre of Cruelty. This proposal for a new theatre was triggered by an event in 1931, when Artaud witnessed a troop of Balinese dancers perform at the Paris Colonial Exposition. He was completely overwhelmed by the idea that this culture used an ancient language of gesture and movement, each action communicating something significant. For Artaud, this was the antithesis of French theatre in which the dominant mode of presentation had been almost exclusively 'verbal', whereas the Balinese were using a 'physical' language of gesture. Artaud quickly set about preparing the way for a new radical theatre to replace the existing 'verbal' European tradition. In two manifestos, Artaud indicated that this new theatre would find a fresh theatrical language consisting of a complex set of gestures, movement and paralinguistic sounds to communicate with the audience. To realise his vision, Artaud specified a number of techniques. His starting point was to reject the traditional play text and formulate a new system for transcribing sounds, gestures, facial expressions and rhythms. For Artaud, conventional theatre was restricted by the limitations of the text in much the same way that his poetry was incapable of communicating his subconscious thoughts. The Theatre of Cruelty rejected social narratives (plays about money troubles, love triangles and so forth) and dealt with boundless subject matter such as ancient myths, creation or the brutality of nature, creating a universal theatre accessible by all. He writes that:

> [By] Abandoning our Western ideas of speech, it turns words into incantation … it breaks away from language's intellectual subjugation by conveying the sense of a new, deeper intellectualism hidden under these gestures and signs …
>
> (*CW4*, p.69)

Evidently, Artaud did not want to remove all text from the Theatre of Cruelty, but simply to reduce its importance so that it was of equal significance to everything else in the theatre space. In this sense, every aspect of a performance must contribute towards the overall intention of the piece.

Alongside the abolition of text, Artaud proposed a restructuring of the theatre business. In an attempt to dismantle the hierarchical creative process, Artaud amalgamated the author, producer and director into a singular role, making one person equally responsible for both action and speech. Similarly, the performer's role was augmented to that of an athletic metaphysician who could summon dark powers in their own body and direct these towards the audience. Through a disciplined training programme, which drew upon a range of Eastern concepts, Artaud asked the performer to express their inner selves through gesture and voice. He demanded that the performer probe beyond their own personality traits in order to reveal the common truths shared by all humans and connect with the spectator on a metaphysical level. In 'An Affective Athleticism', Artaud maintained that all emotional states have physical bases and that the performer must learn to command and manipulate these in order to trigger emotional responses in the audience. Although the essay does not specify how these trigger points should be stimulated, it does identify the importance of breathing as a way to realise the idea. Artaud regarded breathing as a physical manifestation of the body's inner emotional state, and accordingly, the recreation of a breathing pattern could re-trigger its corresponding affection. In particular, Artaud was investing in aspects of oriental belief, whereby the breath is regarded as the essence of existence and creation. Thus, to control one's breath is simultaneously an act upon both the body and the mind. However, Artaud demanded that the performer moves beyond the generation of an experience within their own body and develops techniques to physically project these sensations into the spectator's body. Exactly how this process was to be achieved is unclear, but by discovering powerful vocal frequencies, Artaud hoped that the actor could vibrate and provoke responses in the spectator's body. Similarly, the performer must liberate their inner being through physical gesture, accompanying their vocal performance.

So uncompromising was Artaud's disdain of theatre history and tradition, his Theatre of Cruelty completely dispensed with the theatre building in an attempt to escape its inevitable physical and societal associations. In many respects, the conventional theatre building is emblematic of the Western civilisation that designed it, dividing the audience up into class (stalls, upper circle, boxes) and disenfranchising the general public from the action on the stage both architecturally and aesthetically. Artaud eliminated the auditorium from his designs and hurled the audience into the centre of the theatrical event, unfolding the action around them.

Lighting and sound were vital elements in the Theatre of Cruelty and were required to physically engage the audience, rather than support the action. Artaud called for the inadequate technology of the time to be overhauled and wanted to discover new lighting effects capable of 'playing' with the spectator's mind. Artaud suggested oscillating lights that could be moved, directed and shaped in a way that is not dissimilar to the technology used in modern-day rock concerts. Similarly, Artaud demanded that sound technology be developed in order to find ways of amplifying noises, making them travel and able to 'move' around the space. In his 1935 production of *The Cenci*, Artaud included the following stage direction in the play:

> At times, an amplified sound spreads out, dissolves as if stopped by an obstacle, then is reflected in sharp ridges.
>
> (*CW4*, p.126)

This stage direction is typical of the many sound ideas peppered throughout Artaud's writing and demonstrates how sound is presented as a material substance. Again, the technology imagined by Artaud anticipates modern-day advancements in surround sound, where sounds can be 'placed' in the space and panned from speaker to speaker. Artaud's attitude towards sound, in particular the emphasis he placed upon tonal qualities, is reflected throughout his theatrical proposals, from the retraining of the actor's voice to the invention of new musical instruments from newly-discovered metals.

Artaud believed that by employing the above techniques, the Theatre of Cruelty would be able to disorientate its audience by bombarding the senses of their bodies. By overloading the audience's senses with ear-piercing sounds, pounding drums, rhythmic cries, hypnotic drones and spectacular effects, Artaud hoped that they would be forced into partaking with the performance ritualistically. The objective of this spectacle is to make the spectator feel part of the dreamscape and reconnect them with their own primitive inner self.

Over four years, Artaud developed his Theatre of Cruelty, writing scenarios for productions, manifestos, articles and essays. However, he lacked the financial backing required to stage his proposed theatre. Finally, in 1935, Artaud got a project off the ground, adapting Percy Bysshe Shelley's *The Cenci*, a play based upon a factual account from the 16th century in which a count rapes his daughter and is in turn murdered by her. Under Artaud's direction, the production was a disaster. He found it impossible to communicate his new performance style to his actors, the only theatre available and affordable in Paris was inappropriate for the Theatre of Cruelty and the small budget fell short of meeting the spectacle Artaud was planning. With hostile reviews and a half-empty auditorium each night, the show ran out of money and had to close prematurely after only 17 performances. Disgraced, Artaud hurriedly set about raising funds to flee Paris and, eight months later, left for Mexico.

Whilst abroad, Artaud visited a secluded Indian tribe known as the Tarahumara and joined in with their rituals, specifically one in which the hallucinogenic drug, peyote, was taken. The Tarahumara used peyote to get closer to the forces of nature and to detach themselves from the material world around them through hallucination. Artaud appreciated the parallel between this ritual and the Theatre of Cruelty, removing the audience from the material world and plunging them into a hallucinogenic dreamscape. The ritual had a powerful impact upon every aspect of Artaud's work. For example, during the peyote ritual the Tarahumara would speak in tongues and use ritual screams, ideas reflected in Artaud's productions from the end of his life.

Artaud's mental health and drug addiction was deteriorating by 1937 and after a seven-week trip to Ireland ended in his deportation, Artaud was forcefully admitted into a series of mental hospitals for the next eight years and eight months. In 1943, Artaud was transferred 600 kilometres south of Paris to a clinic in Rodez, which lay outside the Nazi-occupied zone. Although Artaud was materially provided for, his new doctor, Gaston Ferdière, decided to try an experimental treatment on him – electroshock therapy. Artaud loathed the treatment, claiming years later that Ferdière had tried to torture and kill him. It was not until the end of the Second World War and the liberation of Paris from Nazi control that it was possible for Artaud to be released from Rodez. Ferdière had been considering such a release, but wanted assurances that Artaud would be cared for in a Parisian nursing home and would have enough money to last him for the rest of his life. In order to raise money for Artaud's release, friends organised a theatre event and an auction of donated works by a vast number of Parisian artists and writers including Jean-Paul Sartre, Pablo Picasso, André Gide, Tristan Tzara and Marcel Duchamp. Artaud's future was assured and on 25th May 1946 he took the night train back to Paris, where he would live for two more years.

During the final chapter of his life, Artaud worked relentlessly. His poetry, theatre writing, theoretical essays and drawings all merged into a single creative endeavour, all inseparable from his life and his body. More than any other period in his life, Artaud rethought himself as a creative force so strong that it could blur the distinction between different artistic disciplines. For example, his drawings depicted aspects of his theoretical thinking and were scrawled with fragments of poetic text, whilst his performances became interspersed with disjointed fragments of poetry and paraphrases from his theoretical writing.

In 1947, Artaud was asked to produce a long radio broadcast on any subject he desired. Appreciating the artistic freedom that this project allowed him, the broadcast became an accumulation of all of his theories and life experiences. For the first time, Artaud had the chance to reach a mass audience with his views on the corruption of civilisation, religion, language, madness, the body and Tarahumara rituals. Entitled *To Have Done with the Judgement of God*, the broadcast took the form of a long poem, intersected with incoherent babble, violent drumming and Tarahumara screams. Artaud was very excited about the finished recording, claiming that the broadcast was the closest he had ever got to realising his theories on the Theatre of Cruelty – demonstrating how loosely he used the word 'theatre'. The broadcast was set to take place on 2nd February 1948, but the day before transmission, the head of the radio station banned the broadcast on the grounds that it was blasphemous and obscene. Artaud was devastated. In a letter of complaint to the head of broadcasting, his disappointment is evident:

> Permit me to be ... revolted and *scandalized* ... I search in
> vain for the offence it might have caused those well-meaning
> people who had not adopted a stance
> > *in advance* ...

(AT, p.228)

Two days later, Artaud was diagnosed with a fatal intestinal cancer.
The following month, on 4th March 1948, he was found dead, sitting
by his bed. His friends stayed with the body for four days to protect
him from the rats. Antonin Artaud was buried in Paris on 8th March
1948 with a small civil service.

*   *   *

Any biography such as this should conclude with an answer to the
question – 'what did this person achieve?' In the case of Antonin
Artaud, concise answers to such seemingly simple questions are
problematic. Artaud's lifework itself struggles to arrive at an answer
to this question and offers few conclusions or clarifications. In fact,
it is the 'struggle' itself to find new forms of expression in poetry
and theatre that maintains the interest of the modern reader, not the
contradictory answers he sporadically reached. Artaud never achieved
his Theatre of Cruelty and, more frustratingly, never provided a solid
technique for his followers to implement. Nevertheless, he did leave
behind an uncompromising pursuit to discover new forms of
expression, radical visions which have stimulated artists and writers
since his death. As Jerzy Grotowski famously claimed in his 1967
article, 'He Wasn't Entirely Himself':

> The paradox of Artaud lies in the fact that it is impossible to
> carry out his proposals. Does this mean that he was wrong?
> Certainly not. But Artaud left no concrete technique behind
> him, indicated no method. He left visions, metaphors.

It is these vivid, radical visions and metaphors that we will explore
in the following chapters, and where better to start than with Artaud's
most influential book, *The Theatre and its Double*.

Notes

[1] 'Letter to the Chancellors of the European Universities' was co-authored with Michel Leiris. Robert Desnos wrote 'Letter to the Medical Directors of Lunatic Asylums' at Artaud's suggestion. However, Artaud collected it together with his other open letters in his *Collected Works* at the end of his life.

2

The Double

Curiously, Artaud's writing has retained its zeal years after his death, upon numerous re-readings and following critical analysis. Few theatre practitioners have been able to write such complex, multifaceted prose that is capable of propelling the reader from one sentence to the next with such vigour. Although his writing is lively and polemic in itself, this seems unable to account for the intensity and potency emanating from beneath the text. Artaud has concealed an alternative intention in the subtext, expressed discretely through the poetic arrangement of words and ideas, stimulating activity in the subconscious of the reader. Artaud is telling two stories when he writes, one on the surface and one in the subtext – a double.

In February 1938, Artaud published a collection of essays under the title *The Theatre and its Double,* today regarded as the most radical and passionate text ever written about performance. In many ways, this is a problematic book because Artaud never proposed a clear technique or method, claiming in the preface to one essay: "There are enough details for one to understand. To be more explicit would spoil its poetry." Therefore, Artaud intended for these essays to stand as works of art in their own right, not as a manual or a handbook for his proposed theatre. Nevertheless, many modern-day theatre makers, critics and students have turned to *The Theatre and its Double* in search of the blueprint for Artaudian performance. Instead of finding solutions, these readers discover a burning desire to question what theatre is and a radical vision of what performance could be. However, Artaud encountered a dilemma at the point of communicating his vision. Ultimately, he felt compromised if he employed unambiguous text to express his complex ideas, believing that the visceral crux of his vision would be lost to the conventions of language. Therefore, Artaud considered it essential to locate a textual space that was capable of eluding the literalness of conventional language. Consequently, he invested in the subtext. Artaud employed a language dense in metaphor and cataclysmic imagery, likening the Theatre of Cruelty to an 18th-century plague outbreak and the destruction of the biblical town of Sodom from Genesis. These extended metaphors form the "double" to which Artaud referred in the title, *The Theatre and its Double*. He skilfully and vividly presented these doubles as a heightened reality of both his proposed theatre and his worldview, two concepts that were inseparable in Artaud's work. These doubles are complex and textually rich and deciphering them can be complicated. In part, this is due to the rhetoric that Artaud employed, simultaneously attempting to balance the tone of a manifesto (which requires concise, rational statements), an allegory (which demands protracted and sustained symbolism), and that of a passionate, rousing harangue (employing visceral and zealous language). These contradictory surface features of Artaud's text hide a rich and multifaceted subtext that must be examined to understand the true power of *The Theatre and its Double*. In turn, we shall look at the most prominent doubles from the book, starting with the plague.

Plague

The leading essay of the book, 'Theatre and the Plague' begins with striking historical accounts of the virus' affect upon social order and the human body. Artaud tells the story of the *Grande-Saint-Antoine*, a plague-infected ship sailing west across the Mediterranean Sea in 1720. Artaud claims that as the ship sailed close to Sardinia, the plague radiated across the water and touched the consciousness of the Sardinian people. After a vivid dream premonition, the Sardinian Viceroy denied permission for the ship to dock in fear that its hold was infected. So strong was the Viceroy's premonition that he threatened to have the *Grande-Saint-Antoine* destroyed by cannon shot if it approached any closer. The Captain of the ship obeyed and sailed on to Marseilles where he delivered the plague-infected cargo. Over thirteen pages detailing the physical and social effects of the plague pass before Artaud makes the first analogy to theatre, illustrating his technique of sustaining discourse on theatre through allegory. Like Artaud's other doubles, the plague metaphor is designed to elude 'straightforward' explanatory language and capture the imagination of the reader to communicate the point with vigour and power. Unravelling the many layers of this rich and multifaceted essay is a complex task, but a number of emerging themes from the subtext demand attention. Importantly, Artaud spends time identifying the ways in which the plague destroyed the social fabric of Western civilisation, claiming that the moral codes of society "became fluid with the effects of the scourge". The essay euphorically indulges in the corporeal agonies triggered by the virus and recounts incidents of amoral behaviour from plague-struck towns in which social order had dissolved including necrophilia, looting, debauchery and murder. From these accounts, Artaud draws an ideal model for art, equating his new theatre with a plague outbreak. This suggests that the Theatre of Cruelty's objective is to destroy all existing theatre in the same way that the plague consumed whole societies. In this sense, Artaud's ideas on theatre form an all-encompassing revolution that, by affecting the spectator, can spread beyond the theatre building. This leads the critic Robert Brustein to describe the Theatre of Cruelty as a theatre of "revolt", both in the political and adjectival sense of the word. Not only did Artaud want to overthrow the existing theatre and rebuild it in his own image, he also endeavoured to create a theatre that would have a "revolting" effect upon human flesh, where "existence itself becomes the source of his rebellion." Consequently, the spectator is thrown into a state of fear and terror. Although this last idea is essentially poetic, the way in which Artaud intended to physically affect his audience will be discussed in later chapters.

Artaud's imagery raises the characteristics of the plague microbe beyond scientific classification, engendering the virus with a consciousness and a motive. In the text, Artaud taunts science's inability to comprehend the plague by revealing inconsistencies in their infection-through-contact hypothesis. He maintains that the virus was capable of 'selecting' its victim and that science was unable to explain the extraordinary geographical spread of the plague. Further, Artaud described the resulting social behaviour as a 'symptom' of the viral infection, curiously suggesting that the plague is not simply spread physically through contact, but also psychologically through the human psyche. This explains how the

Sardinian Viceroy was able to pick up 'vibrations' of the plague from a ship that had not physically docked in his country and how hysteria spread through infected towns. Artaud's account undermines the fundamental scientific principles that underpin Western civilisation, questioning the reader's confidence in such beliefs.

A sizeable proportion of the essay is allocated to identifying the corporeal effects of the plague, revealing how the body is affected from the inside out. Artaud tells us that although the disease under the skin may burst through the surface of the flesh in the form of buboes, it is the internal putrefaction of the inner organs that brings about death. He makes a direct link between the flesh and wider society, comparing the plague's affect upon the body to the natural forces shaping the landscapes of the planet. Thus, Artaud draws no distinction between subjects when he writes, simultaneously 'doubling' his views on society, theatre and corporeality. He regards the body as one of Western civilisation's institutions. Through Western science, our concept of the body has become medicalised and safe, divorcing it from nature and our primitive, animal roots. Consequently, the flesh of the body has imprisoned human thought. (For example, to verbalise thought, one must use their voice organs; to see and hear, one must use their sense organs.) However, Artaud felt that he had something to say that went beyond the body's limited abilities and the plague metaphor offered him a chance to 'pierce through the flesh' and achieve mental freedom. Although this idea may seem idealistic, it does provide the poetic basis upon which to interpret Artaud's ideas. Like the plague, the Theatre of Cruelty disrupts the civilised constructions built up around the spectators' bodies, enabling them to attain mental freedom. By abolishing the perspectives imposed upon society through science, religion, law, culture and political ideologies, the Theatre of Cruelty is simultaneously the death and cure of Western theatre.

In seeking a new concept of performance, Artaud sought external influences, an idea 'doubled' in the plague allegory. According to Rodolphe Gasché's remarkable, yet often overlooked essay, 'Self-Engendering as a Verbal Body', we can find the arrival of this external influence in the subtext of 'Theatre and the Plague'. The ship that brought the plague to Marseilles was called the *Grande-Saint-Antoine*, which, when read aloud in the original French, contains a double meaning (the essay was originally written for a public lecture at the Sorbonne in 1933). *Grande* translates as 'big', *saint* when pronounced in French is sonically the same as *sein* meaning 'womb', and *Antoine* when pronounced in French is sonically similar to Artaud's Christian name, 'Antonin'. Literally, Artaud writes that the plague is carried in the "big-womb-of-Antonin" and is delivered to his birth-town of Marseilles. Metaphorically, Artaud himself carries the virus that will destroy existing theatre. As Artaud noted, the plague brought by the *Grande-Saint-Antoine* was the most lethal of all – the Oriental virus.

Oriental theatre

The Theatre of Cruelty was reportedly triggered by an incident in 1931. In this year, Paris held a colonial exposition in which an ambitious series of performances from around the French Empire were presented. In particular, Artaud saw a troop of Balinese dancers who revealed a performance language free from the Western reliance upon realism. The narrative was presented through a complex vocabulary of gestures, cries, postures, hypnotic drumming and music that responded to the action, all of which appealed to Artaud's artistic project. He considered the effect upon the Parisian audience to be an emotional rediscovery of a primal, lost language from which the Western audience had become divorced (but were perhaps still able to emotionally engage with). Although Artaud was unable to decode the complex sign system behind the gestures, he was overwhelmed by the intensity of the performance. His emotional state was reflected in his animated review published a few days later. This text is a fervent piece of writing that rejects the expected literary conventions of performance criticism, instead capturing Artaud's personal viewing experience in all its visceral richness. As Artaud becomes mesmerised and lost in the performance, the writing also becomes increasingly fragmented. Short separated sections of text offer 'glimpses' of the performance interwoven with Artaud's own thoughts. One short section describes the look of a dancer's eyes, another, the effect of the trance and frenzy upon Artaud's mind, abandoning literary structure altogether. Eventually, a reworked version of this review was incorporated into *The Theatre and its Double* under the title 'On the Balinese Theatre'.

After reading this essay, it may seem contradictory to discover that, in reality, Artaud had little interest in Balinese dance and that he misunderstood and misreported many of the Oriental performance techniques. Surprisingly, Nicola Savarese informs us that Artaud did not, in fact, witness an ancient dance passed down through generations, but rather, a comparatively modern dance choreographed as a counteraction to Bali's religious tradition. Instead of idealising the performance, the objective of 'On the Balinese Theatre' was to prove that conventional Western theatre is merely a style of performance to which we have become accustomed. As the critic Susan Sontag notes in her seminal essay 'Approaching Artaud', "the stimulus could just as well have come from observing the theatre of a Dahomey tribe or the shamanistic ceremonies of the Patagonian Indians. What counts is that the other culture be genuinely other; that is, non-Western and non-contemporary." Therefore, it seems that Artaud's interest in Balinese dance was more of strategic importance than influential. Beyond appreciating the underlying principles of Oriental theatre, Artaud had no desire to reproduce Balinese performance techniques in the Theatre of Cruelty. Instead, he highlighted the mere existence of such a radically different theatre as an opportunity to question the West's reliance upon realism and propose new aesthetic possibilities.

At its core, Oriental performance provided evidence that the link between literature and theatre was a social convention, not an artistic necessity. Artaud believed that the importance placed upon the play text by Western theatre makers was misguided and that all critical analysis was simply conducted upon literary terms, ignoring the very theatricality of performance. Thus, Artaud sought to reinvent the role of the text, transforming it from a predetermined production blueprint into a stimulus for performance. He hoped that such a break from literary forms would interrupt intellectual responses to theatre, devoid of emotion and 'life', and enable visceral experiences.

Painting

Artaud begins the essay 'Production and Metaphysics' with a vivid description of Lucas van Leyden's 1609 painting, *Lot and his Daughters*. This painting depicts the Old Testament story from Genesis in which God destroys the town of Sodom for its corrupt behaviour. The narrative unfolds episodically in the painting; in the far background, the town of Sodom can be seen, its church spire toppling, the buildings crumbling into the harbour alongside the wreckage of merchant ships. In the blackened sky above the town, the cause of the catastrophe can be seen; red-hot hail and brimstone cut through the dark clouds from heaven. On a rickety wooden bridge, leading away from the devastation, the silhouettes of Lot and his daughters are visible, fleeing the catastrophe. In the foreground, we find Lot and his daughters taking refuge in the mountains later that night. One daughter is sitting on her father's lap, the other pouring wine. Although the painting does not explicitly depict the incest of the bible story, the events are anticipated in its composition.

Why did Artaud place such importance upon this painting? He tells us that "this painting is what theatre ought to be, if only it knew how to speak its own language", and consequently, we can find all of the elements that constitute a Theatre of Cruelty upon its canvas. Evidently, there is a link between Artaud's views and Leyden's depiction of the destruction of a corrupt civilisation through metaphysical means (in this instance, the hail and brimstone replaces the plague metaphor). In addition, the boundless subject matter contained in the painting would have appealed to Artaud, composed of incest, fate and genocide. However, Artaud's fascination goes deeper than an aesthetic appreciation of the painting's surface features. He senses something deeper, a force emanating from behind the oils on the canvas. Upon viewing this painting in the Louvre, he claims to have been mesmerised by the inferno in the sky, the fireworks leaving streaks in his eyes, suggesting to him that dark powers radiate from the canvas. This exuberant analysis tells us little about the painting itself, but rather more about how Artaud constructs his doubles and how to interpret them. When viewing *Lot and his Daughters*, Artaud was reading the subtext, the subconscious of the painting. Artaud's own writing 'doubles' this and his Theatre of Cruelty operates on a similar latent level, pushing language beyond its literal boundaries.

One startling factor that leaps from 'Production and Metaphysics' is Artaud's exclusion of Lot's wife from his analysis, whereas she is focus of the original bible story. Lot's wife had been warned by God's angels to flee the town of Sodom and not to look back. However, halfway through her escape, she could not resist her curiosity and turned to see the destruction of her home. She instantly halted and her flesh turned to salt. In Leyden's painting she is faintly visible, a tiny silhouette with her arms outstretched, frozen on the crumbling wooden bridge before the catastrophe. Although Artaud never makes explicit reference to her, the tone of the essay presumes that the reader has some prior knowledge of the biblical story, and therefore the image of Lot's wife turning into a pillar of salt would be present in the subconscious of the reader. She drifts through the subtext of 'Production and Metaphysics', but never surfaces directly into the text. Martin Harries suggests that Lot's wife takes on metaphorical status and represents the spectator in the Theatre of Cruelty. She becomes "the icon of the spectator who has already looked back ..." having seen a vision so overwhelming that it physically affected her flesh. Again, there is a metaphorical link with Artaud's plague imagery, depicting a force so cruel that it acts upon the body.

If not a theatre of text, then the Theatre of Cruelty is a collage of archetypal images often drawn from biblical sources. For example, the shipwrecks from *Lot and his Daughters* resurface in *The Conquest of Mexico*, the destruction of civilisation is visualised in *The Spurt of Blood*, and the image of a daughter pouring wine for her incestuous father reappears in *The Cenci*. By referring to such archetypal images, Artaud hopes to bombard the senses of the spectator and get 'under the skin' – the same experience endured by Lot's wife. Thus, the literary criticism of the past becomes redundant and a new method of analysis must be devised to account for the Theatre of Cruelty's visual format.

Cruelty

Cruelty is Artaud's most dynamic, yet ambiguous double. Although in *The Theatre and its Double* Artaud specifically dedicates an essay to the idea, 'Theatre and Cruelty', it stands distinct from the other doubles. Instead of taking the form of an allegory, cruelty functions as an overarching metaphor capturing the essence of the other doubles. Although the term formed the title of Artaud's Theatre of Cruelty, he used the word elusively and was often misunderstood. A common misinterpretation of the term is to invest in its connotations with bloodshed and butchery. Such an analysis is understandable considering Artaud's employment of distressing images in 'Theatre and the Plague'. Equally, some supporters considered the word too restrictive and unable to convey the ambitiousness of Artaud's artistic project. In *The Theatre and its Double*, Artaud included two letters to his publisher, Jean Paulhan, defending his use of the term:

> This cruelty is not sadistic or bloody … [and] must be taken in its broadest sense, not in the physical, predatory sense usually ascribed to it … [I demand a] return to the etymological origins of language, which always evoke a tangible idea through abstract concepts.
>
> (*CW4*, p.77)

Artaud's attitude towards language is consistent in every respect, not only adopting the rhetoric of the double for his allegories, but also for his definitions. Like the plague, the reader must delve beneath the conventional surface of the word "cruelty" and examine its connotations to discover its poetic core.

Artaud employs the term 'cruelty' in four ways: 'cruelty as essence', 'cruelty as discipline', 'cosmic cruelty', and 'cruelty as theatrical presentation'. The first meaning presents cruelty as the driving force behind all human behaviour, as the essence that underpins everything we do. As Artaud succinctly states in 'Theatre and Cruelty', "Everything that acts is cruelty", employing the term metaphorically to describe the exhilaration of all human experience. This idea has been indirectly borrowed from Friedrich Nietzsche, a German-born philosopher writing at the end of the 19th century. His definition of cruelty informs Artaud's own, declaring that all art embodies and intensifies the underlying brutalities of life to recreate the thrill of experience. For Nietzsche, tragedy extends beyond its literary boundaries and describes the peculiar aspect of human nature which enjoys the adrenaline of self-suffering. Below, I have quoted extensively from Nietzsche to illustrate the striking parallels between the two writers:

> Almost everything we call 'higher culture' is based on the spiritualization and intensification of *cruelty* … That which constitutes the painful voluptuousness of tragedy is cruelty; that which produces a pleasing effect in so-called tragic pity, indeed fundamentally in everything sublime up to the highest and most refined thrills of metaphysics, derives its sweetness

solely from the ingredient of cruelty mixed in with it. What the Roman in the arena, the Christian in the ecstasies of the cross ... the Parisian workman who has a nostalgia for bloody revolutions ... – what all of these enjoy ... is the spicy potion of the great Circe 'cruelty' ... its origin [is not] in the sight of the sufferings of *others:* there is also an abundant, over-abundant enjoyment of one's own suffering ...

Artaud's own conception of cruelty seems to have been borrowed verbatim from Nietzsche, even appropriating his rhetoric to illustrate how the cruelty of life should be incorporated into the theatre. Although Artaud did not formally cite Nietzsche, the rhetoric in the passage above contains a familiar persuasive authority, a similar exuberant phraseology, and motifs *in extremis* suggestive of Artaud's own writing. For example, in 'No More Masterpieces' Artaud prefigured his discussion on cruelty by claiming that theatre has become disconnected from life, illustrating the point with catastrophic images similar to Nietzsche's:

the masses tremble at railway disasters, are familiar with earthquakes, plagues, revolutions and wars ... the masses today are thirsting for mystery.

(*CW4*, p.57)

It is cruelty that provokes Artaud's distinctive use of catastrophic imagery, implying that his fundamental objective for the Theatre of Cruelty was to recreate life's most visceral experiences.

Here, a contradictory meaning emerges also borrowed in part from Nietzsche: 'cruelty as discipline'. Artaud wrote that "cruelty means strictness", a statement which seems to contradict the notion that the Theatre of Cruelty aimed to 'unleash' dark powers, reject form and incite chaos. However, Artaud also appreciated the rigour in developing a performance technique. For example, it was the precision of the Balinese dancers that Artaud admired, which in turn influenced his recommendation to develop new ways of transcribing movement, sound and vocal inflection with exacting detail. Hence, the chaotic stage images Artaud envisaged were to be made up of smaller, tightly-directed components, merely creating the effect of anarchy. We can see this technique at work by comparing the script and prompt book from his 1935 production of *The Cenci* (dealt with in detail in Chapter 4). The third scene requires "Confusion. GUESTS … rush about, panic-stricken, advance as if into battle", yet the prompt book and its accompanying blocking diagrams demonstrate that this was achieved through strict choreography. Every performer moved in formation to exact cues, circling around each other, spiralling in and out of the action, and forming "whirlwind" shapes. Thus, Artaud uses the term cruelty to express the level of control and discipline required to realise his theatre proposal.

A third use of the term, 'cosmic cruelty', confirms the link between Artaud's theatre and his wider understanding of human existence, or "Everything that acts …" Evidently, Artaud's view of the universe is stark indeed with no virtuous God to protect or morally guide us. In an early text, 'On Suicide', Artaud described life as a series of chance accidents causing a perpetual state of suffering, perhaps an idea inseparable from his own ill health. He explains that death is the only way to take control of one's destiny and escape the absurdities of life. This is reflected in 'Theatre and the Plague' where death is presented as a relief from society and a 'setting free' from materialism. The victims' torturous purgatory between life and death constitutes a 'real' vision of being for Artaud and it was this cosmic certainty that Artaud wanted to reveal to his audience. If the cosmic laws that dominate human existence are cruel and unchangeable, then theatre should reflect this. Thus, Artaud used the term cruelty as both a "double" of the stark realities underlying human existence and the process of revealing these to the masses.

This leads us to the final meaning of the term: 'cruelty as theatrical presentation'. For Artaud, the separation between reality and theatre is characterised by aesthetic distance. Watching the now infamous scene from Edward Bond's *Saved*, the spectator is not compelled to intervene or flee in search of help when a child is stoned by youths. Similarly, we do not feel complicit in Macbeth's murder of Duncan. From these examples, it is clear that aesthetic distance emotionally paralyses its audience, rendering them passive and inert. For Artaud, this is a theatre divorced from the realities of life, lacking passion, danger and possibility. Thus, Artaud sought to remove aesthetic distance, bringing the audience into direct contact with the dangers of life. By turning theatre into a place where the spectator is exposed rather than protected, Artaud was committing an act of cruelty upon them.

Although Artaud may have spent much of his time denouncing organised religion, the double reveals a deeply spiritual streak in his proposed theatre. Artaud's cruelty is a form of ritual, a ceremony in which both spectator and performer partake. In doing so, Artaud shared a practice with organised religion, witchcraft and magic. He suggested that the conventions of traditional theatre (character, trivial plots and so forth) be replaced by a performance of rites establishing a spiritual bond between the spectator, the performer and the cosmos. Artaud envisaged a ritual powerful enough to throw the spectator into a trance and reveal the stark realities of human existence.

*   *   *

This chapter has explored the doubles most commonly associated with Artaud's work. However, the list is not finite. Although Artaud had loosely used the term before, the concept of the double, as used today, was an afterthought. In fact, the title for *The Theatre and its Double* was only decided in the final editorial stages of the publishing process. Therefore, the double does not exist as a specific writing technique or a theory per se, but rather as a way of characterising Artaud's approach.

The double is an active concept. It is a way of breathing life into a dead theatre, hijacked by the literary cannon and perpetuated by commercialism. Additionally, the double enables Artaud to speak about his theatre as if it were living, as if it were in the present. Without the double, the Theatre of Cruelty remains conceptual.

3

The Disease of the West

From the outset, the Theatre of Cruelty was to be a useful theatre. Artaud envisaged a theatre of alchemy, a place where the spectator could be permanently transformed and where a mass encounter could cure society of its ills. Unsurprisingly then, the scope of Artaud's polemic spills across the boundary that separates art and reality, unleashing his scorn upon capitalism, the church, science, culture, language, tradition and political ideology. Making connections between these objects of Artaud's contempt leads to a common denominator – they are all the products of Western civilisation. However, Artaud seemed more interested in the dark forces that lie beneath the surface of civilised society. For him, true freedom was to recognise and connect with the spiritual forces that shape our existence:

> [The Theatre of Cruelty] unravels conflicts, liberates powers, releases potential and if these and the powers are dark, this is not the fault of the plague or theatre, but life.
>
> (*CW4*, p.20)

Evidently, Artaud's spiritual beliefs were a far cry from the comforting Christian view, suggesting that his perception of the spiritual forces at work in the universe are evil and "dark".

Many critics, most notably Susan Sontag and Jane Goodall, have described this philosophic attitude towards Western civilisation as Gnostic. Broadly speaking, Gnosticism diametrically separates the spiritual and physical realms, claiming that the latter is a corrupted outgrowth from the former. The presence of evil in the world leads the Gnostics to question the 'goodness' of God, concluding that the material world had in fact been created by a demiurge; a demonic being who created and introduced evil into the physical world. Importantly, both Artaud and the Gnostics endorsed the dualism between the spiritual and physical realms, considering the latter to be evil, materialistic and fake. Throughout *The Theatre and its Double*, Artaud uses the term Western civilisation to describe this corrupt physical 'outgrowth' and impresses his conclusions upon the reader in no uncertain terms:

> Now to my mind the present state of society is iniquitous and ought to be destroyed ... All the topics detailed above stink of mankind, of materialistic, temporary mankind, I might even say *carrion-man*.
>
> (*CW4*, p.29)

A disease that has eliminated the natural forces of nature from our "iniquitous" society has infected the whole of Western civilisation. In the above passage, he calls this disease "carrion-man", using the double meaning of the word "carrion" to simultaneously describe the iniquity of the material world and the cycle of social decay – the more we abide Western civilisation, the more steadfast it becomes. Artaud understood this cycle to be a disease capable of permanently divorcing humankind from their spiritual essence and proposed a remedy in the form of theatre.

Artaud believed that Eastern cultures had been less infected by this disease than Western ones, consequently investing in a range of Oriental practices and ideas. In his investigation of Artaud's appreciation of Oriental ideas, 'Eclecticism, Oriental Theater and Artaud', Rustom Bharucha identifies the psychological differences between the Eastern and Western mind. He notes that in the West there is a tendency to fragment knowledge, encounters and passions into categories, which creates a distorted perception of human experience. This idea is reflected in Western theatre where plays are presented and critiqued upon cultural, economic and philosophical frameworks. In comparison, Eastern theatre reflects the wholeness of the Oriental disposition, appealing to the entire being in a direct, non-literal way. In the East, Artaud discovered an emotive form of performance to remedy the 'intellectualised' theatre of the West. Thus, the Theatre of Cruelty becomes inseparable from the pains and passions of life. Bharucha notes:

> One of the inexorable axioms of the Theater of Cruelty is that theater cannot be seen apart from existence. It is no longer a question of art mirroring life since art is buried in the innermost regions of human consciousness. Artaud is not merely fascinated by the technique of Oriental theater but, more significantly, by the Oriental state of mind, the consciousness that permeates its artistic creations.

By appealing to the entire being through art, Artaud wanted to reconnect the physical and spiritual world. In this sense, the Theatre of Cruelty sits upon the boundary between these two realms, acting as a gatehouse through which the Western spectator may be reconnected with their own spiritual essence.

At this point in exploring Artaud's ideas, many readers 'jump ship' because they cannot bring themselves to conceive of the world in the same way. In actuality, the essence of Artaud's theatre is lost without a 'leap of faith' from the reader. However, Artaud's gambit is not a shallow concept employed to give his writing a mystical tone, but is derived from one of philosophy's oldest questions. Therefore, a review of Artaud's ideas on the spiritual and physical realms is required to dissect his work and reveal the central premise threading throughout his writing and thinking.

The Leap of Faith

Artaud was apprehensive about the synonymous link between the terms 'spiritual' and 'religious' in the West. He insisted that the two terms are acutely separate concepts and felt compelled to find a more accurate phrase to describe his spiritual, yet secular ideas. Ultimately, he employed the term 'metaphysics' to describe the spiritual realm. Although Artaud disliked the word for its vagueness and ethereal connotations, he did consider entitling his project the Metaphysical Theatre. In a letter written in 1932 to Jean Paulhan, Artaud admits that he replaced the title with the Theatre of Cruelty because those who did not share his philosophical beliefs would ridicule it. The term continued to hamper Artaud's writing process and his trepidation stopped him from ever attempting a clear definition of his use of the word. Therefore, we must examine the term 'metaphysics' in its broadest sense. This particular branch of philosophy investigates the possible existence of a realm beyond material experience (*meta* deriving from the Greek for 'beyond'). In constructing its perception of physical existence, the human brain does not come into direct contact with the world outside its body. Instead, it creates a 'mental impression' of its material environment from the sense-data collected through the flesh. Immanuel Kant's illustration of this process noted that humans do not directly 'see' the external world in three dimensions, but that the illusion of three-dimensional sight is cerebrally constructed. Each eye organ is only capable of capturing a two-dimensional image and generates a nerve impulse to communicate this to the brain. Upon receiving the impulse, the brain decodes it and merges the two images to create the impression of three dimensions. In this way, all human perception is cerebrally constructed, and consequently, the breadth of experience is restricted to the physical limitations of the body's senses. It is therefore possible that certain sensations have been circumscribed from our worldview. These 'un-sensed' experiences are metaphysical and Artaud wanted to bring his spectators into contact with them.

Artaud realised that many Eastern and ancient societies incorporated the spiritual into their worldviews. Therefore, he suspected that the contemporary Western mind had been taught to reject metaphysical impulses. By creating a theatrical experience designed to undermine the foundations of Western civilisation, exposing it as nothing more than a material fabrication, Artaud hoped his audience would rediscover the metaphysical experiences of their pre-civilised ancestors.

Again, there is a strong Nietzschean influence in Artaud's philosophic approach. He, like Nietzsche before him, was suspicious of the logical, rational human thought that underpinned and produced Western civilisation. He also seemed to appreciate the Nietzschean idea that logic does not exist outside the brain, but is in fact constructed by it. In *The Gay Science*, Nietzsche asked, "Whence did logic come into existence in the human head? Certainly out of illogic, whose realm must initially have been tremendous." Although Nietzsche did not attach the same importance to the metaphysical realm as Artaud did, there is a sense that he makes a similar distinction between the logical, material world and the illogical, metaphysical realm. For Nietzsche, the physical environment surrounding the body is not the creation of a divine architect, but rather, it has been "willed" into being by the human instinct to construct order from the natural chaotic world around us. Furthermore, Nietzsche's belief that language perpetuates and strengthens this fabrication by artificially ordering and simplifying raw illogical experiences is reflected in Artaud's deep mistrust of the written word, declaring its inability to communicate his most primitive and metaphysical thoughts. Although Artaud never formally recognised Nietzsche, the parallels between their thinking are uncanny, both aiming to expose the way in which civilisation is constructed.

The Theatre of Cruelty sits between logical constructions, between the physical and metaphysical, corruption and purity, evil and good. This theme of transgressing the boundaries between concepts separated in the Western mind threads throughout all of Artaud's work. He is a shadow, a spirit drifting in the space between chaos and order, and he asks his actors and spectators to accompany him. If Artaud can convince us to take the 'leap of faith', to follow him and to see the world as he does, then he may stand a chance of 'de-civilising' us and unveiling our primitive selves. For Artaud, the exposure to metaphysical forces in theatre would break the cycle of "carrion-man", forcing society to re-evaluate its achievements.

But surely, Artaud's theatre is impossible? It is a theatre that rejects form, yet the materiality of space, objects and bodies constitutes the basis of all performance practice. Artaud's compulsion to pursue the extremes of his philosophy impeded his theatrical model. To achieve a metaphysical state, Artaud demolished all theatrical and social conventions. So unconditional was his revolution that he also proposed dispensing with human flesh. In *To Have Done with the Judgement of God*, he advocated a "body without organs" to suggest that the body is only a temporary state of being. In a letter written in 1946 to an English publisher, Artaud claimed that he had died more than once in his life. Notably, during the Tarahumara peyote ritual and whilst undergoing the rudimentary electroshock therapy at Rodez. He described these deaths as 'out of body' experiences, transgressing beyond his material flesh and, for a short time, occupying the metaphysical realm. Such images reoccur throughout his work and serve as a reminder of his belief that material corporeality is not an absolute requirement for existence. In a lecture delivered at the University of Mexico-City in 1936, Artaud described how life and the body are not two interdependent concepts:

> 'But that is metaphysics, and we can't live in metaphysics.'
> So what I am saying precisely is that life must be restored
> into metaphysics, ... *to be simultaneously* in death and in life.
>
> (*AT*, p.150)

The plausibility of this concept must remain at the discretion of the reader, but its importance in deciphering Artaud's work must not be underestimated. During his time in Mexico, Artaud found parallels between his theory and the belief systems of the indigenous people. In the same lecture, he drew upon this parallel to explain how he perceived metaphysics as an external space:

> Culture is a movement of the mind which passes from the
> void to forms and from these forms returns to the void as to
> death. To be cultured is to burn down the forms, burn down
> the forms to achieve life. It is to learn to stand upright amidst
> the continual movement of forms which are successively
> destroyed.
> The ancient Mexicans never knew any other approach than
> this passing to and fro between death and life.
>
> (*AT*, p.149)

In this passage, Artaud stands beyond culture (synonymous with Western civilisation and the physical realm) watching these temporary, material states take form and disperse. This vantage point can only be located in the metaphysical realm, a place where he exists without physical form. Through his theatre, Artaud hoped to escape his own body and enable his spectators to similarly 'remain erect' in the metaphysical realm.

Artaud's uncompromising approach placed his ideas in direct opposition to Western institutions, whose function is to maintain the logic of civilisation. Artaud believed that the most insidious of these organisations is the church which, by revering God as an emblem of goodness, is able to justify all other secular ideas as evil. Consequently, the church is able to maintain moral control over the masses by judging the morality of all actions upon their own self-authored doctrine. In an early text, 'Manifesto in Plain Terms', Artaud states his refusal to acknowledge the relationship between good and evil because the distinction can not be found in nature. He understands morality to be a social construction and a method of controlling the freedoms of the masses. This idea informs 'Theatre and the Plague' where the disease and the ensuing social anarchy dissolve all logical structures (including good and evil). Interestingly, the inhabitants of the plague-infected towns evaded judgement upon their amoral acts, precisely because the moral framework used to reach such a verdict had been destroyed in the catastrophe. It follows therefore, that a primary objective of the Theatre of Cruelty was to replace civilisation's 'moral judgement' with 'moral freedom'.

Artaud attempted to identify the mechanisms of moral control. What he discovered had a heavy impact upon his aesthetic project and became a source of great suffering throughout his artistic life – it was the very words that he employed to express himself which maintained the system he wanted to destroy. Thus, he turns his scorn upon the institution of language.

Rediscovering the Thought before the Word

> Writing is all trash.
> People who leave the realm of the obscure in order to define whatever is going on in their minds, are trash ... Those for whom certain words and modes of being have only one meaning ... those who classify feelings and ... believe in "terms" ... are the worst trash.
>
> (*Collected Works, Volume 1*, p.75)

Here, Artaud is asserting that language is incapable of communicating beyond a superficial level, reducing complex mental experiences into "terms". Thus, Artaud's dilemma was that to express himself he must use the "dead" words of others. By insisting that words must be given plural meanings, Artaud depicts conventional language as a random association of sounds with objects and concepts, beyond which meaning breaks down. In a humorous passage from 'Production and Metaphysics' in *The Theatre and its Double*, Artaud ridicules Western civilisation's dependence on such meaningless language:

We all agree a beautiful woman has a pleasing voice. Yet if from when the world began we had heard all beautiful women call us by snorting through their trunks and greet us by trumpeting, we would ever after have associated the idea of trumpeting with the idea of a beautiful woman and part of our inner vision of the world would have been radically changed.

(*CW4*, p.29)

Artaud's understanding that language is unstable on a semiotic level leads to the characteristic sense of anxiety which pervades in his writing, an anxiety which attracted the attention of Jacques Rivière at the start of Artaud's career. After initially rejecting Artaud's poems, Rivière's interest was reignited by Artaud's account of the anguish experienced during the writing process – to find words capable of expressing his deeply metaphysical thoughts and feelings. The anomaly of a writer accounting for the inadequacy of his own unprintable poems triggered Rivière's curiosity. A correspondence between the two men was soon underway during which Rivière attempted to support and guide the young Artaud into developing a coherent writing style, advising in one letter that "With a little patience … you will be able to write perfectly coherent, harmonious poems." However, Rivière misinterpreted Artaud's aesthetic stance – Artaud's failure to express himself becomes the very 'subject' of his writing. The extent to which Rivière understood the significance of the correspondence is debatable. On one hand, Rivière urged Artaud to express himself coherently, whilst on the other, it was the correspondence itself (the documentation detailing Artaud's failure) that Rivière finally published. In his first letter to Rivière, Artaud claimed, "I suffer from a fearful mental disease. My thought abandons me at every stage." Thus, the struggle evident in all of his prose and poetry derives from the need to give form to his inner thought and discover his own "intellectual being".

Artaud could feel the presence of civilised constructs operating in his head, separating himself from his primitive spirit. The moment a metaphysical thought emerged, the civilised part of his mind attacked it, divided it up into logical fragments and, in the process, destroyed its essence. This was followed by the act of writing where the words available to him suddenly seemed inadequate to convey the plurality of life's experiences:

> This brings us to call into question the language of the spoken
> word as it is currently conceived in Europe, as a means of
> expression, and to ask whether it fulfils all the organic
> essentials of life.
>
> (*AT,* p.134)

As a writer, Artaud became a prisoner of the text without the means
to express his pre-linguistic thought. He attempted to either push the
written word to its very limit or sidestep language altogether to
capture the thought before the word. Thus, the Theatre of Cruelty
championed a new flexible language of sound, inflection, screams
and cries in an attempt to overcome conventional representation.

Artaud's paradox stimulated the direction of Jacques Derrida's
own post-structuralism. Through a number of close textual analyses
of Artaud's writing, Derrida demonstrated the unstable relationship
between language and meaning. He drew attention to Artaud's use
of the word "subjectile", a term with no singular meaning of its own,
but amalgamated from others (including 'subject', 'projectile' and
'subjective'). Derrida uses Artaud as a platform for his own
philosophy and is interested in exposing the artificiality of
representation and language. Thus, Derrida understands Artaud's
"subjectile" as an attempt to sidestep the act of representation and
acknowledge the 'original' impetus behind language. He wrote that
Artaud "kept himself at the limit of theatrical possibility, and …
simultaneously wanted to produce and to annihilate the stage",
demonstrating his appreciation of Artaud's (unsuccessful) attempt
to eliminate mimesis from theatre.

Similarly, Julia Kristeva's important contribution to literary
analysis has been triggered by Artaud's desire to give form to the
thought before the word. Based upon her reading of Artaud, she
argued that the pre-verbal instinct is transmogrified during its
"expulsion" from the body. Therefore, all objects become separated
from their subjects, placing language and thought in disharmony
with each other. For both Kristeva and Derrida, language becomes a
material manifestation from which the individual has absented. What
both thinkers appreciated in Artaud's writing was his struggle to
overcome the separation caused by representation and maintain
presence in his texts.

This chapter has attempted to locate the nucleus of Artaud's writing. What we have uncovered is a struggle to escape the materialism of Western civilisation. The Theatre of Cruelty embodied this struggle, proposing a transgression from the physical to the metaphysical realm. If Artaud can achieve this, then he can successfully deflate the authority of Western civilisation's oppressive structures – law, morality, Christianity, language and the body. Artaud's attitude towards the body is of particular importance, claiming that corporeality was a by-product of civilisation rather than a prerequisite for existence. Hence, he demanded that the body undergo a poetic purgatory, a burning of the flesh to remove the boundary between the physical and metaphysical self. This idea is evident in 'Theatre and the Plague', where Artaud concentrates on the virus' affect upon the human body, the buboes ripping open the flesh from the inside out. Artaud spares no pity for the victims, instead euphorically celebrating their new-found freedom.

However, the extent to which Artaud's philosophy is translatable into performance practice is debatable. The Theatre of Cruelty is a means to an end; a device to disrupt the fabric of society. Thus, it supersedes art and becomes a form of communion and a rite of passage. I ask a question: to what extent is theatre suited to his quasi-philosophical objective? In truth, there is a gulf between Artaud's philosophy and theatre practice, and the latter compromises his vision.

Even the most ardent Artaud enthusiast must accept that his successes were vastly outweighed by his failures, an unfortunate aspect of his work that demands an objective exploration.

4

A Failed Vision?

It is unfortunate that Artaud's theoretical work exceeded his praxis. Although he considered himself a practical man of the theatre, his applied Theatre of Cruelty amounted to little more than a small handful of productions, each with their own complications. Consequently, Artaud's theatrical vision remained conceptual, communicated solely through essay, manifesto, scenario and play text. It was not until more than a decade after his death that practitioners such as Peter Brook and Richard Schechner finally realised his ideas on theatre, but in his own lifetime Artaud fell short of his aims. His essays and manifestos promised something much more magnificent than his projects delivered, questioning the extent to which his ideas on theatre were achievable and realistic.

Critical assessments of Artaud's praxis have fallen into two distinct camps. Firstly, there are those that identify a fundamental flaw in Artaud's worldview. The Theatre of Cruelty was designed to bring its audience into contact with metaphysical impulses, but Artaud did not sufficiently explicate this idea. If Artaud's Gnosticism was misplaced, then his theatre was constructed upon a false premise. Secondly, some believe that Artaud's failure can be attributed to the limitations imposed upon him professionally and personally throughout his life. Whichever argument is accepted, the same conclusion is reached – Artaud's theory is not reflected in his practice.

This chapter will attempt to address this inconsistency by reviewing some of Artaud's most important practical projects and assessing the extent to which he compromised his theories. It is unfortunate that some plays remain incomplete or lost altogether. *The Burnt Womb, or the Mad Mother* was staged in 1927 for the Theatre of Alfred Jarry and *The Torments of Tantalus,* an adaptation of Seneca's play, was completed in 1935 but never performed. Both texts are missing. The loss of *The Burnt Womb, or the Mad Mother* is particularly regrettable because it is one of the few texts performed during Artaud's lifetime. Similarly, Artaud attempted to enact a cosmic cataclysm in a scenario entitled *There is no more Firmament*; this text remains incomplete and in three very different drafts making an objective reading problematic. Furthermore, I would like to remind the reader before embarking that Artaud was an interdisciplinary writer. His work stretches across the fields of poetry, theatre, film, critical essay, biography and fiction. Combined with the disruptions caused to his artistic life by his mental health and drug addictions, it is very difficult to consolidate these various fragments of writing into one voice. As his main achievement has been the influence he exerted over modern-day theatre, I will restrict myself to exploring his major performance-based projects, an approach taken by most critics in this field.

The Spurt of Blood

Written in 1925 for the Theatre of Alfred Jarry, *The Spurt of Blood* is a tiny play consisting of little more than a few pages of text. Consistent with the other work produced for this theatre, *The Spurt of Blood* owes its roots to the surrealist movement, from which Artaud was expelled shortly after writing the text. The fabric of this short play unfolds like a dream, each surrealist image melting into the next. The play is a vivid nightmare, depicting the destruction of civilisation and an act of vengeance from God. However, the 'double' of the play reaches further than this, the imagery depicting a cosmic cruelty. As the following synopsis reveals, the play unleashes a series of extreme, nightmarish images upon the audience, bombarding their senses and attacking society's moral codes.

It begins with a young man and a young girl declaring their love for each other, an event that triggers a colossal cosmic disaster. It transpires that these star-crossed lovers are also brother and sister, the incestuous act disrupting the natural order. Two stars are seen to collide above their heads, signalling a cosmic upheaval. A terrifying noise fills the theatre and, from the explosion, dismembered body parts descend from the sky in slow motion. The downpour of human limbs is followed by the ruins of Western architecture, including "colonnades, porticoes, temples and alembics, falling slower and slower as if through space ..." A Wetnurse enters followed by the Knight who demands some papers which are buried deep in the Wetnurse's pockets. Finally, she throws the Knight his papers from which he produces Swiss cheese. The Young Man, having lost his lover, is met by the Priest whose faith is in crisis. He asks, "What part of her body did you refer to most often?" to which the Young Man replies, "To God". Disconcerted by this, the Priest confesses that his spiritual role amounts to little more than wallowing in the small petty crimes of his parishioners, a reflection of Artaud's view of the church. The absurdity of the Priest's role being divorced from spirituality is highlighted by the Priest's accent changing to Swiss in an instant.

Without warning, the stage is plunged into darkness and frenetic flashes of lightning zigzag their way across the space. Picked out in the light of the flashes are the characters, running in terror and colliding with each other. From this chaos emerges an image which is both blasphemous and farcical. A giant hand reaches down from the heavens and grabs one of the characters by their hair. God's hand has picked the Whore whose hair immediately bursts into flames signifying the collision between two very different moral orders. The Whore's dress becomes transparent, revealing a disgusting body beneath. To escape God's grip, the Whore bites the wrist sending a huge spurt of blood across the stage. This sacrilegious crime signifies the end to all logical order and the scene plunges into darkness again. When light returns, we are met with the aftermath of the Whore's blasphemy – she stands lustfully in the arms of the Young Man surrounded by corpses. The Wetnurse returns and lifts her dress to reveal a swarm of scorpions running up and down her legs whilst her vagina swells and splits, glistening like the sun. The final image of the play is the Young Woman waking to discover her lover suspended in the air. Cryptically, she remarks, "The Virgin! Ah, that's what he was looking for."

It is difficult to identify an appropriate perspective from which to examine *The Spurt of Blood*, especially when it is considered that the elaborate synopsis above has been drawn from a play covering less than four pages. Paule Thévenin, the person who knew Artaud most intimately and left with the mammoth task of collating and editing his life's work, described the play as an example of his sardonic humour. She claims that the play was a parody of Armand Salacrou's *The Glass Ball,* a little-known text published around the same time in a French periodical. Although it is true that four characters in *The Spurt of Blood* have been directly lifted from Salacrou's play, they are represented as distorted mirror images of themselves. For example, in *The Glass Ball* there is indeed a young couple who declare their love for each other, a knight who picks up sweetie wrappers from the floor and a wetnurse who is searching for a young woman. However, in *The Spurt of Blood* Artaud has hurled these characters into an unstable dreamscape and removed the conventional structures of Salacrou's play, yet retaining certain abstract fragments. In typical style, *The Spurt of Blood* operates through a complex web of contradictions, decentralising the characters further by placing their intentions at odds with their actions. As Albert Bermel notes in his study of the play, the Priest admits that he has no faith, the Young Man seeks a virgin, but ends up in the arms of a bawd, and his father (the Knight) displays only the vestiges of masculinity. Even God appears vulnerable and bleeds like a human.

As I mentioned above, the imagery in *The Spurt of Blood* depicts a cosmic cruelty, suggesting that the play also violates the audience's worldview. The play rejects Western civilisation on many levels. Notably, the opening scene is set in the physical realm, presenting a world of order, rules and convention. When declaring his love, the Young Man exclaims, "Ah, what a well-made world". This line immediately precedes a 'cruel' disruption to the ordered world where emblems of the physical realm fall from the sky. The stage becomes littered with human flesh and Western architecture, literally depicting the fallout of the destruction of the material world. This explosion has been caused by a major rupture to conventional moral frameworks – the incest of the lovers/brother and sister. Artaud often returns to incestuous themes in his writing, appreciating the 'cruelty' of the crime, its perpetrators obeying their primal sexual desire at the expense of civilised rules. From this turning point, the spectators are forced to partake in the dreamscape, their senses bombarded with unstable and unpredictable images. The Whore's hair bursts into flames, her dress becomes transparent, scorpions swarm upon the Wetnurse's legs whilst her vagina swells and splits, the Young Man is suspended in the air and a giant hand reaches down from the heavens. All of these images are designed to de-civilise the audience's perspective, bringing them closer to a metaphysical experience.

Whilst vivid, the text was not produced until 1964. Even today, the lavish effects demanded by the stage directions would be technologically and financially testing, but in 1920s Paris, these acts of spectacle were certainly beyond the capabilities of the existing theatre. There is little evidence to suggest that Artaud seriously pursued this project practically, and therefore we must ask ourselves, 'why did Artaud write it?' Was it an experiment or purely an act of parody aimed at Salacrou's *The Glass Ball*? Although Artaud may have been aware of the limitations of this play and the impossibility of staging it in 1925, it does mark a brave departure from the existing playwriting tradition. However, the play embodies a dilemma that would return to plague Artaud in future projects. In written form, *The Spurt of Blood* appears considerably shorter than its running time. This is because the stage directions demand elongated sequences of action and it is from the 'silences' between the short, clipped dialogues that the real possibilities of the play emerge. We can also see Artaud developing techniques to place importance upon the tonal qualities of the performer's vocal delivery, rather than upon the dialogue itself. He does this by preceding most dialogue with delivery instructions specifying the intonation, pitch, pace and intention behind each line. The practical difficulties of writing *The Spurt of Blood* must have either identified or confirmed this dilemma to Artaud. To write for theatre, his text must take the format of a script which Artaud considered incapable of conveying the fundamental elements of theatrical performance – action, image and emotion.

The Philosopher's Stone

Written in 1929 but never performed, *The Philosopher's Stone* falls into the limbo between the collapse of the Theatre of Alfred Jarry and the development of a Theatre of Cruelty. Consequently, it contains elements of both projects. The strong sense of parody and surrealist imagery carries over from *The Spurt of Blood,* but is countered by Artaud's new experimental approach towards theatre writing. The text employs a scenario format to communicate the theatrical vision rather than the conventional play text (as was the case with *The Spurt of Blood*). Artaud splits the text into sections (set, characters, plot and development), providing a framework for a devised approach rather than offering a predetermined blueprint for the production.

Essentially, the text presents the tried-and-tested tale of the cuckolded man through surrealist imagery. Doctor Pale is an alchemist searching for the philosopher's stone, an imaginary substance that could turn base metals into gold. In the opening scene, the doctor is wielding an axe, chopping human flesh like a butcher. On the other side of the stage sits his wife, Isabelle, described by Artaud as unable to "imagine love assuming any other form than this frigid doctor – and love leaves her unsatisfied". Isabelle has been completely dominated by Doctor Pale, their relationship depicted through physical movement. Doctor Pale's movements are echoed by Isabelle, reacting to each blow of the axe as if it were striking her own flesh, smiling when her husband smiles, and so on. Her feelings towards her husband are evident during their morose sexual intercourse during which Isabelle's clumsy sexual advances towards the doctor are countered by her disgust of him, slapping and scratching at his body.

Meanwhile, Harlequin enters – a virile young man who desires Isabelle. He has a scheme with which to steal Isabelle away from Doctor Pale, presenting himself as a trembling, half-sighted hunchback. However, when the doctor turns away, Harlequin stands straight and makes physical displays of his virility to Isabelle, who is overcome with sexual ecstasy. Harlequin announces his pretext for entering the house: "I HAVE COME TO HAVE THE PHILOS-OPHER'S STONE TAKEN OUT OF ME." This statement consumes Doctor Pale partly with scientific interest and partly with greed, but the ruse is discovered and the doctor dismembers Harlequin in the laboratory.

Later, when Doctor Pale is sleeping, Harlequin's torso begins to move. It gathers its limbs and its head and reforms anew. He crawls towards Isabelle and the two begin a flirtatious series of gestures which end with Harlequin drawing his hand up the inside of Isabelle's leg. They are discovered by Doctor Pale who begins advancing upon them menacingly. Hurriedly, Harlequin and Isabelle engage in exuberant animalistic displays of courtship, jumping into the air and shaking themselves. They reveal a child, a perfect miniature copy of Doctor Pale, who realises that he must be its father. He and Isabelle embrace.

Unlike *The Spurt of Blood*, *The Philosopher's Stone* completely rejects dialogue as the primary vehicle for presentation. Only two lines are assigned to the characters throughout the entire scenario and Artaud disengages these from the speaker. As the on-stage performer mouths the words, the lines are delivered from the wings creating a sense of dislocation. Artaud reduces the importance of language further by investing in the sonic qualities of the dialogue rather than its textual meaning. For example, pauses and delivery instructions pepper Harlequin's only line:

> "I HAVE COME TO HAVE THE PHILOSOPHER'S STONE
> TAKEN OUT OF ME." … *in a quavering, accented voice.*
> A short pause after "I have come"; long after "stone"; longer
> still and indicated by a stop in movement on "of me".
> *(Collected Works, Volume 2*, p.75)

The influence of surrealism upon this scenario is clear, but the images have more coherency than those contained within *The Spurt of Blood*. Artaud is telling a somewhat conventional story here, drawn from the tradition of *commedia dell'arte,* a physically demanding form of improvised street theatre popular between the 16th and 18th centuries. Widely travelled, *commedia dell'arte* troupes developed a physical approach to storytelling which overcame language and dialect barriers, an idea that clearly resonated with Artaud. Furthermore, *The Philosopher's Stone* resurrects the stock characters from *commedia dell'arte*, but each with crueller dispositions. Artaud presents Harlequin, the most distinctive of all *commedia dell'arte* characters, complete with his mischievous schemes and comic mimes (alternating between a bandy-legged hunchback and a virile young man). Similarly, Isabelle's flirtatious and headstrong nature is borrowed directly from the *commedia dell'arte* character of the same name. Pantalone, her father, is the counterpart to *Il Dottore* who is always attempting to control and dominate her life, also reflected in *The Philosopher's Stone*. Finally, Doctor Pale also mirrors the familiar role of *Il Dottore*, the pedagogue who is outwitted by the lower-class characters.

What did Artaud hope to achieve by writing *The Philosopher's Stone*? It is unclear whether he attempted to modernise, parody or pay homage to *commedia dell'arte*. Certainly, he did not completely abolish the internal structure of the art form, as he had done with Salacrou's *The Glass Ball*. Instead, Artaud retained and developed some of the essential elements including the physical approach, the stock characters and the scenario format. We must consider the context in which this scenario was written – Artaud still had the desire to overturn conventional performance practice, but the collapse of the Alfred Jarry project had left him 'theatreless'. Therefore, I see this project as an experiment in form, anticipating the Theatre of Cruelty. In a number of letters to the theatre director Louis Jouvet in April 1931, Artaud reflected upon the Theatre of Alfred Jarry's fundamental pitfall. He concluded that its actors were not sufficiently disciplined in the art of improvisation and was concerned that this may reflect negatively upon his abilities as a practitioner. Thus, Artaud sent *The Philosopher's Stone* to Jouvet in an attempt to reinstate his reputation as a practical man of the theatre. Alas, Jouvet did not share his enthusiasm for an avant-garde reworking of a traditional art form and *The Philosopher's Stone* was never staged in Artaud's lifetime. A few months after his correspondence with Jouvet, the Paris Colonial Exhibition opened and Artaud saw the troupe of Balinese dancers that triggered his conception of a Theatre of Cruelty. With the identification of a new artistic direction, *The Philosopher's Stone* became redundant.

The Conquest of Mexico

Artaud never developed *The Conquest of Mexico* beyond a detailed scenario, but it demands attention because it contains many of the elements essential for the Theatre of Cruelty. Interestingly, Artaud used the scenario as if it were a promotional document for his new theatre, incorporating it into his manifesto and giving a public reading of the text in 1934 to raise funds. Although he claimed that it was to be the first production of the Theatre of Cruelty, he never completed a full manuscript or staged it from scenario format. Whilst this failure can be attributed to a lack of funds, it may also be the case that Artaud himself realised how truly ambitious this project was.

The scope and breadth of the subject matter in *The Conquest of Mexico* is epic, dealing with Hernando Cortez's conquering of Mexico in 1519. Artaud envisaged a four-act production that would depict the clash of two societies, the 'civilised' Spanish and the 'primitive' Mexican Indians. Despite its historical context, Artaud was denouncing modern-day Europe, attempting to undermine the spectator's faith in Western civilisation by exposing the aggression and corruption used by 'civilised' cultures to occupy and conquer the world's 'natural' societies. He hoped that the subject matter would connect with the modern world:

> [*The Conquest of Mexico*] revives Europe's deep-rooted self-conceit in a burning, inexorably bloody manner, allowing us to debunk its own concept of its supremacy ... It treats the false conceptions the West has somehow formed ... with the contempt they deserve ...
>
> (*CW4*, pp.97-8)

To achieve this, he excluded the conventions of domestic drama and demanded that every aspect of the performance embody this clash of civilisations. The result is a vision which operates on a 'total' level, staging "events rather than men".

In this sense, the yet-unconquered Mexican landscape becomes the subject of the majority of the first act. The terrain itself, visualised through lighting effects and music, anticipates the catastrophe that will soon engulf it. At first, a sense of unease creeps over the land where everything "shudders and creaks ... A landscape which senses the approaching storm," followed by a building frenzy of activity. Wind effects, lightning, projected shadows of bolting horses and the amplified sound of a discontented populace fills the stage. Only then does Artaud introduce the actors, suggesting that they are a material manifestation of the terrain. On one side of the landscape, we see Montezuma emerge, the Aztec Emperor surrounded by his priests, and on the other side, the Spanish army assembles, led by Cortez. Behind the conquistador, Artaud places an image which is strikingly similar to the biblical destruction wrought in the painting *Lot and his Daughters* (discussed in Chapter 2):

> On Cortez's side, a *mise en scène* of seas and tiny, tossed caravels, and on a grander scale Cortez and his men, as solid as rocks.
>
> (*AT*, p.92)

In the second and third acts, Artaud skilfully presents the differing worldviews of both Cortez and Montezuma, employing a remarkable duel-perspective technique. In Act Two, we see the colonisation of Mexico through the eyes of Cortez, his Western psychology filtering his experience. Act Three replays the same events through Montezuma, who is receptive to the metaphysical forces of nature and the cosmos. Where Montezuma perceives disarray and massacre, Cortez perceives order. Where Montezuma hears the screech of swords being sharpened and the screams of warriors in battle, Cortez rejects this experience, hearing only "a muffled muttering, full of threats, [and] an impression of awesome solemnity ..." The gulf between 'primitive' and 'civilised' psychology is at its most acute in Montezuma's and Cortez's perception of a magical ritual. Artaud describes in detail the lavish ceremony that enables Montezuma to connect spiritually with his people and the Gods:

> Magic, magical *mise en scène* of an evocation of the Gods ... The wall of the stage is crammed unevenly with heads, with throats: cracked and strangely sliced melodies, answers to these melodies appear truncated. Montezuma himself seems split in two, appears double ... with faces painted on his body like a multiple meeting point of consciousness, but from within Montezuma's conscience all the questions are transmitted to the crowd.
>
> (*AT,* p.92)

In Act Two, Cortez witnesses this same event, but his perception is devoid of any spiritual context. By rejecting all metaphysical impulses, his Western mind only allows him to see the "magic of a motionless dumb show ..."

In the final act, Montezuma is abdicated and murdered, an event which unsettles the natural order. Montezuma's leadership was both spiritual and political, and consequently, the social fabric of Mexico is seen to disintegrate. Again, this is evident upon the Mexican landscape as the metaphysical life is drained from it, "crushed like watery fruits squashed on the ground". The terrain throws up images iconic of this new 'civilised' dynasty. Murder, rape, betrayal and looting replace the peaceful serenity evoked in Act One, but all with the underlying possibility of a revolt.

The Conquest of Mexico is a stark, unremitting piece of writing and its link with contemporary Western civilisation is unambiguous. In this sense, the text marks a transition in Artaud's writing from his surrealist roots to the development of a tightly-focused aesthetic of 'cruelty'. Whilst there is a similar juxtaposition of images as there had been in *The Spurt of Blood* and *The Philosopher's Stone*, Artaud refined the technique in *The Conquest of Mexico*. The images which make up the four acts are chosen and interwoven with greater ingeniousness than in previous works. Similarly, the filtering of experiences through Eastern and Western perception (in the Nietzschean sense) is a unique and complex presentational device. Alas, Artaud could not raise the funds for this project and it did not become the first production of the Theatre of Cruelty. Instead, he developed a four-act play to launch his theatre, entitled *The Cenci*.

The Cenci

In 1935, Artaud directed his only full-length theatre production, *The Cenci*, which ran for just 17 performances before it financially crashed. Many critics believe that the play compromised Artaud's ideas on theatre because it employed a conventional literary structure. Whilst I concede that *The Cenci* was a deeply-flawed project, I think that an examination of the play is still worthwhile and is able to deepen our understanding of the Theatre of Cruelty. By looking beyond the written text itself and considering the original objectives of the 1935 production, it is possible to build up a useful picture of Artaud's praxis.

For *The Cenci*, Artaud adapted Percy Bysshe Shelley's play of the same name, which he in turn based upon a historical account from the state archives in Rome (also the source for Seneca's play). The narrative concerns a 16th-century count who is presented in Artaud's text as a malevolent force of evil intent upon undermining society's moral order through the crimes that he commits. Artaud wastes no time in establishing the moral frameworks that operate in the text, opening the play with a conversation between Count Cenci and Camillo (who has just defended him in a meeting with the Pope). In an intentional break with the naturalism of the time, Artaud has Count Cenci outwardly declare his innermost impulses rather than allowing the character to be psychologically motivated. He reveals that his only aim in life is to commit a final act of horror and that he has already planned this ultimate crowning glory. As a cardinal of the church, Camillo endeavours to dissuade him, insisting that he should conduct his life within the acceptable moral frameworks of Christianity, but Count Cenci refuses to repent his sins or to acknowledge the Pope's authority:

> There is no life, no death, no God, no incest, no contrition, no crime in my existence. I obey my own law, of which I am my own master ...
>
> (*CW4*, p.123)

The Nietzschean sentiment is evident in this passage. Count Cenci occupies his own moral space beyond the confines of good and evil, a theme woven throughout the play. For example, to celebrate his 'good news', Count Cenci threatens the moral order by announcing a taboo orgy for the nobility of Rome. Further, to visualise this debauchery, Artaud made explicit reference to Paolo Veronese's painting *The Marriage Feast at Cana,* which depicts the bible story where Jesus turns water into wine. Evidently, viewing this mammoth painting in the Louvre left its mark upon Artaud. Perhaps the vast scale of the canvas fascinated him, where on viewing, the scene fills the spectator's field of vision and draws them into the action as if joining the multitude of guests. Although there may be a clear link between the 'total' experience of viewing this painting and the audience experience in the Theatre of Cruelty, it is more probable that Artaud's appreciation derived from Veronese's reputation as a sacrilegious artist. *The Marriage Feast at Cana* places a solemn religious scene within an incongruous Roman setting, the canvas vibrating with hedonistic exuberance. This is evident in the attire and conduct of the guests and the lavish architecture that frames them (itself reminiscent of a 16th-century theatre). This irreverent combination of decorum and ostentation is typical of Veronese's enthusiasm for biblical storytelling, an enthusiasm not appreciated by Venice's growing Catholic orthodoxy. Consequently, Veronese was called before the Inquisition in 1573 to account for the irreverent content of his painting *The Feast in the House of Levi*, a canvas similar to *The Marriage Feast at Cana* in terms of theme, scale and composition, and was instructed to make alterations. Artaud, well versed in art criticism, would have undoubtedly been aware of Veronese's skirmish with the religious authorities and may also have appreciated that the alterations demanded by the Catholic church were never made.

Once the guests have assembled at the start of Act One, Scene 3, Count Cenci reveals the event they are celebrating. He raises his goblet of wine (which has religious connotations through the subject matter of the painting) to toast the death of his two sons. The count then proceeds to contort moral order out of all recognition by claiming that God had answered his prayers for infanticide; that the ultimate Christian force had ordained this sacrilegious crime.

Count Cenci's daughter, Beatrice, becomes fearful of the fate her father may be plotting for her, but is unable to escape from the castle. The third act begins with an inconsolable Beatrice revealing that her father has rapped her in order to condemn her spirit to eternal damnation. With the help of Orsino and Bernardo, Beatrice plots her revenge and hires two mute assassins to murder her father. Only upon the second attempt are the assassins successful, but whilst Count Cenci lies bleeding in his bed, the plot is disrupted by Camillo who demands to speak with the count. Beatrice, caught red-handed, is arrested for her crime. In prison, Beatrice finally comes to the 'cruel' realisation that it is impossible to escape destiny. She is fated to be tortured by her father; either her blood father or the pope in his capacity as father of the church:

> BEATRICE
> The Pope's cruelty is as great as old Cenci's … It is
> wrong that fathers should unite against the families they
> create. Nor have I had a chance to present my defence
> before the father of Christianity.
>
> CAMILLO
> Did you give your father a chance to present his before
> you butchered him?
>
> (*CW4*, p.151)

Here, Artaud is suggesting that Count Cenci's evil acts are synonymous with those of the church and that, whilst their moral integrity may differ, their cruelty is comparable.

Artaud's use of the performance space is of particular interest in

The Cenci, reflecting his proposal that the Theatre of Cruelty should spatially disorientate the spectator. The stage directions reveal a number of devices designed to dislocate the audience from their physical environment and engulf them in a world with its own spatial principles. To achieve this, Artaud employed indeterminate settings throughout. The majority of the action does not take place in the public spaces of Cenci's castle, but in nondescript spaces such as deep winding galleries, bedrooms, wastelands and stairwells. As the play advances, Artaud increasingly removes all points of reference, forcing the spectator to question their own spatial perception. For example, in Act Two, Scene 2, Artaud creates a hallucinatory effect to disrupt the complacency of the spectator:

> [As Camillo and Giacomo] talk, they appear to be walking,
> but they travel less distance than normal.
>
> (*CW4*, p.136)

This stage direction attempts to transpose dream imagery to the stage and create physical movement that disrupts accepted spatial principles. Similarly, at the end of the third act, the stage space is engulfed by a crescendo of action, literally flooding the senses of the audience:

> The ASSASSINS instantly burst forth … two booming pistol
> shots ring out. Night falls. The lightning stops. Everything
> disappears.
>
> (*CW4*, p.143)

Artaud emphasises the volatility of the theatrical landscape in *The Cenci* by contrasting turbulence with silence. However, this innovative form of presentation remained unaccomplished in the 1935 production and Artaud failed to realise his vision.

It is curious that *The Cenci* employed such a conventional narrative, a predictable use of character and a strong reliance on text-based language. In this respect, the text appears to embody the traditional theatre that Artaud wished to destroy. A host of circumstances surrounding the difficult production of *The Cenci* may have culminated in its failure. For example, funds were hard to raise and Artaud had to accept patronage from a wealthy Russian family on the condition that their daughter, Lady Iya Abdy, could take the part of Beatrice. Begrudgingly, Artaud agreed despite her weaknesses as a performer. Furthermore, the production went over budget, Artaud had to compromise on many of the effects he had planned, and he had tremendous difficulties in communicating his complex theatrical ideas to his mostly inexperienced cast. In addition to these problems, the only theatre available was the Folies-Wagram, a music hall venue that was architecturally inappropriate for staging the Theatre of Cruelty. Despite this vast catalogue of justifications, it is impossible to escape the fundamental flaw that lies at the heart of the script itself; although thematically consistent with Artaud's ideas, it was not capable of realising his performance practice. This disparity leads Sontag to the conclusion that Artaud's praxis remains essentially poetic:

> *The Cenci* is not a very good play … and the interest of his production of *The Cenci*, by all accounts, lay in ideas it suggested but did not actually embody … He has exerted influence through his ideas about the theatre, a constituent part of the authority of these ideas being precisely his inability to put them into practice.

Interestingly, there is evidence that Artaud may have been aware of the shortcomings of *The Cenci* and we should briefly consider his reasons for embarking upon a project that he knew might compromise his theatrical vision. In an article published shortly before the production opened, Artaud stated that *The Cenci* "is not yet the Theatre of Cruelty but is preparing the way for it." Perhaps Artaud did not intend *The Cenci* to be a fully-rendered example of his performance praxis, but instead wanted to create a 'public forum' through which he could highlight the themes and ideas underpinning the Theatre of Cruelty. Roger Blin, who worked closely with Artaud during the project, supports this. He claimed that Artaud only intended to introduce some of his ideas in preparation for his vastly more ambitious project, *The Conquest of Mexico*:

> *Les Cenci* was for him only a means toward making the public aware of some of his ideas concerning *The Theatre of Cruelty*; concerning the word, gesture, certain little-known musical traditions … Artaud hoped that the success or the half success

of *Les Cenci* (for him it was only a half-way point toward his real goal) would enable him to raise enough money to present his next production, the one he dreamt of, his scenario of *The Conquest of Mexico*.[1]

The Cenci was reviled by critics and audience numbers soon diminished. Despite his frantic work to raise funds, the production collapsed on 21st May 1935, leaving Artaud artistically humiliated and financially destitute. Seven months later, Artaud fled Paris and travelled to Mexico by boat where he hoped to rediscover his passion for a 'primitive' theatre. If he could not bring *The Conquest of Mexico* to Paris, then he would take the Theatre of Cruelty to Mexico. Although Artaud did not engage in any practical projects during this time, he did deliver a series of lectures on theatre which were subsequently printed in the Mexican press. However, *The Cenci's* failure and the subsequent humiliation deeply affected Artaud and he never attempted a theatre project again.

To Have Done with the Judgement of God

After his nine-year ordeal interned in French asylums, Artaud returned to Paris in 1946 a broken man. Although he would only live for two more years, this period proved to be creatively charged. He was commissioned by Radiodiffusion Française to produce a radio broadcast on whatever subject he desired, the final recording a culmination of his life's efforts. Artaud decided on the title *To Have Done with the Judgement of God* for the final broadcast, itself reminiscent of Nietzsche's maxim, "God is dead". The title cuts to the core of Artaud's conviction, championing a society free from religious moral frameworks.

The broadcast takes a series of performance poems and intersects them with extended sound sections consisting of screaming, drumming and crude 'songs' played upon xylophones. The result is a complex, layered recording employing sound and text to launch an aural attack upon the listener, engaging them in a sound-rite akin to a primitive ritual.

Artaud himself performed the opening text, rallying against the dangers of America's growing materialism. The second text, 'Tutuguri: The Rite of the Black Sun', provides an account of a

Tarahumara dance which is held up as an antidote to America's repulsive social practice. The following two texts both concentrate upon the body. In text three, 'The Search for Fecality', Artaud's own mortality is horrifically revealed to him when he realises that his physical form is wasting away. In the fourth text, 'To Raise the Question of …', Artaud considered the effect that his physical death would have upon his spirit. Is his spirit condemned to rot alongside his flesh, forever remaining a prisoner of his diseased body, or can his spirit escape "space,/time,/dimension" and enter the metaphysical realm, here described as "infinity"?

The opening text berates American materialism with an incredulous story of a state-sanctioned practice in American public schools. Upon enrolment, Artaud claims that each male child must donate a little of their sperm to an artificial insemination factory where America is cultivating a synthetic army to defend its "false manufactured products". Although conceived in 1947, Artaud's image of America's insatiable consumerism is deeply prophetic of today's materialist world. He wrote:

> glorious true nature will just have to withdraw,/and give up its place once and for all and shamefully to all the triumphant replacement products, / … No more fruit, no more trees, no more vegetables, no more ordinary or pharmaceutical plants and consequently no more nourishment,/but synthetic products to repletion.
> (*Wireless Imagination: Sound, Radio and the Avant-Garde*, p.311)

This passage resonates closely with a host of modern controversies surrounding the lack of nourishment in processed foods, genetically modified crops and so on. Significantly, Artaud views materialist American culture as a growing force in *To Have Done with the Judgement of God*, revisiting the themes in the broadcast's closing text. Entitled 'Conclusion', the text takes the form of a poetic conversation between Artaud and Gaston Ferdière, his psychiatrist from Rodez. Here, Artaud stated that one of the purposes of the radio broadcast was to denounce the American people "who occupy the entire surface of the former Indian continent …" Artaud's choice of the word "surface" is interesting here, suggesting that he viewed

American culture as a synthetic membrane unfolding across the land, region by region, smothering the natural ancient Indian culture beneath it. As we have seen, metaphors such as these thread throughout all of Artaud's writing, reflecting his belief that the material physical world is an outgrowth from the natural metaphysical realm. Artaud suggested that America's materialism is affecting individuals both mentally and physically. As the inhabitants of the West consume the synthetic products of American culture, their bodies also take on synthetic features, divorcing themselves from nature. This metaphor connects each of the texts in *To Have Done with the Judgement of God*, and Artaud's own expiring body emerges as the subject of the performance.

'The Search for Fecality', the third text, conveys the pain and anguish felt by Artaud within his own body, possibly resulting from a deadly, undiagnosed intestinal cancer:

> In order to have shit,/in other words meat,/where there was only blood/and scrap-iron bones/and where there was no question of earning being/but where there was a question of losing life.
>
> (*WI*, p.316)

The tone of this passage reflects Artaud's horror at his loss of control over his own digestive system, his faeces and blood highlighting his own mortality. He claims that the meat from his body is literally dripping through his digestive system, reducing him to a man of "scrap-iron bones". Artaud's fear stems from the dread that his metaphysical being, trapped inside his perishing body, may be destined to rot alongside his dying flesh. Leo Bersani believes that Artaud's spiritual terror is activated at the moment when he sees his "body's waste pass through the anus and to see that waste is to witness a decomposition (a separation of matter from life) to which another passing through or dropping away originally and irrevocably doomed us."

Throughout *To Have Done with the Judgement of God,* Artaud rejects his mortal physical form. Instead, he desires a metaphysical existence; a body without material form; a "body without organs". He declares:

> [Mankind must] undergo … a session on the autopsy table in
> order to remake his anatomy … When you have given him a
> body without organs, / then you will have … restored him to
> his true liberty.
>
> (*WI*, p.328-9)

Here, Artaud is pleading for immortality and a separation of his
thought from his flesh. The key to unravelling Artaud's "body without
organs" is to examine the scream-scapes that litter *To Have Done
with the Judgement of God*. They convey a visceral connection
between both performer and listener. Artaud's screams are textured,
emotive and expressive. They lunge forth and then retreat to the
silences; they echo from a distance and then cascade around you in a
range of varied tones from the beautiful to the terrifying. The screams
amalgamate to form a dense, volatile language more capable of
communicating Artaud's corporeal pain than any words. There is a
sense of 'projected' pain in the recording, the energy of the sounds
metaphorically recreating Artaud's body in the mind of the listener.
Occasionally, the recording transcends this metaphor and projects
Artaud's corporeal pain literally onto the nervous system of the
audience, where 'sharp' sounds pierce the ear, replicating the pain
caused in Artaud's body when producing the scream. In this sense,
Artaud's corporeal pain can still be felt when listening to the
recording, each scream literally projecting his now dead body through
time and space. Even listening to the recording today, many decades
after Artaud's physical flesh has perished, one still gets a sense of
Artaud's body emerging from the sounds. The screams are so visceral
that they cannot be disassociated from the body that produced them.
For Artaud, the objective was to project his physical body into the
sounds of the broadcast, thus transcending the material limits of his
flesh and become a "body without organs".

Upon completion of the editing, Artaud was delighted with the
recording. He claimed that he had finally created a performance which
acts upon the audience's nervous system "with vibrations,/which call
upon/man/TO COME OUT/WITH/his body/and follow in the sky
…" Evidently, Artaud felt that he had at last achieved his Theatre of
Cruelty, believing that the recording could enable his audience to
move beyond their physical bodies and 'move in the sky'.

Although it may not be possible to confirm that Artaud literally managed to transcend his corporeality in *To Have Done with the Judgement of God*, it does seem that the project worked poetically and metaphorically. Tragically, the day preceding transmission, Artaud's triumph was banned on blasphemous grounds by the head of Radiodiffusion Française, who replaced it with a pro-American documentary. Despite Artaud's devastation and the public scandal that ensued, the ban remained in place and the recording was not heard on French radio until 30 years after his death.

*   *   *

Examining Artaud's praxis is a frustrating task. His successes were obstructed by material circumstances rather than creative ones, yet these projects remain the only way of assessing the practicability of the Theatre of Cruelty. For example, Artaud never managed to stage *The Spurt of Blood*, *The Philosopher's Stone* or *The Conquest of Mexico*, and so we can merely speculate upon their production techniques. Similarly, *The Cenci*, by Artaud's own admission, was not a fully-rendered presentation of his proposed theatre. Moreover, *To Have Done with the Judgement of God* was banned the day before transmission. Naturally, many commentators have concluded from this that the Theatre of Cruelty does not translate into practice. Whilst there is undoubtedly some truth in this statement, I would also argue that, due to the circumstances which surround these projects, they are inappropriate texts upon which to judge the validity of his theories.

In searching for a competent method of evaluation, writers like Martin Esslin focused upon Artaud's life, maintaining that the key to understanding his work is to contextualise it biographically. As we have discovered, Artaud literally attempts to project his life-force into his texts. He imposes his own moral frameworks upon Count Cenci (playing the part himself in the 1935 production), his corporeality emerges from the screams in *To Have Done with the Judgement of God*, and his own name is buried within the verbal subtext of his essay, 'Theatre and the Plague'. As Sontag astutely notes, the relationship between Artaud's writing and life moves beyond an aesthetic parallel. For Artaud, the act of writing is the manifestation of thought, and therefore the text becomes an inseparable part of his consciousness:

> In Artaud's poetics, art (and thought) is an action ... and
> therefore a passion, of the mind. The mind produces art ... art
> is the compendium of consciousness, the reflection by
> consciousness on itself, and the empty space in which
> consciousness takes its perilous leap of self-transcendence.

There is no separation between Artaud's writing, body and thought, viscerally attaching himself to both language and subtext. Consequently, his body becomes the very subject of his writing. For example, when Artaud read 'Theatre and the Plague' at the Sorbonne in 1933, he felt compelled to embody the corporeal agony he was describing. The following recollection of Artaud's lecture-cum-performance, from his close friend Anaïs Nin, is especially telling:

> To illustrate his conference, he was acting out an agony ...
> His face was contorted with anguish, one could see the
> perspiration dampening his hair. His eyes dilated, his muscles
> became cramped, his fingers struggled to retain their flexibility.
> He made one feel the parched and burning throat, the pains,
> the fever, the fire in the guts. He was in agony. He was
> screaming. He was delirious.

Many of the texts collected together in *The Theatre and its Double* were written for public lectures and therefore Artaud's praxis stretches beyond the handful of projects examined in this chapter. Artaud refused to recognise the boundaries between different types of text, projecting his life-force and corporeality into every pen stroke. If a primary aim of the Theatre of Cruelty was to collapse the boundary between reality and art in a corporeal, visceral way, then each project is a personal triumph for Artaud. When Artaud's body contorts with the agonies of the plague, or when Count Cenci's dialogue stumbles into reciting whole sections from Artaud's polemic essays, the boundary separating his life and work becomes impossible to locate.

Notes
[1]   This interview with Roger Blin by Charles Marowitz was reprinted in 'Antonin Artaud's *Les Cenci*', *The Drama Review* (June 1972, Vol. 16, No. 2). Please see the bibliography for more details.

5

Exploring Artaud

As we shall discover, Artaud's influence upon contemporary theatre practice is compelling. Although he essentially failed to realise the Theatre of Cruelty before his death, the polemic he left behind resonated powerfully with the 1960s counter-culture. It is through reviewing this 'Artaudian renaissance' that the full extent of Artaud's influence upon theatre becomes clear. Without such an investigation, the link between Artaud's theory and practice is deeply unsatisfying.

After his death, Artaud's theories laid dormant in the English-speaking world for over a decade. If he intended for the Theatre of Cruelty to be a useful theatre, then his Gnostic attacks upon mediocrity and materialism, and his demands for social change through the body had fallen out of favour. During his lifetime, the relationship between the body and the state had been resolute, but the huge social and cultural upheavals between the late 1950s and early 1970s demanded a repositioning of this boundary. By 1956, public discontent was an international affair, fuelled by Britain's role in the Suez Crisis, the Soviet's violent suppression of the Hungarian Revolution, and the brutal crushing of the Poznań Protest by the Polish Communist government. Throughout the 1960s, a growing tolerance of sexuality (both heterosexual and homosexual) flourished alongside the political situation, demanding that the body be liberated from state control, hence the maxim championed by the new wave of feminism: "The personal is political". Through protesting and the more promiscuous sexual practices of the British and American people, the physical presence of the body as a social and sexual weapon was brought to bear upon the political sphere.

In searching for a new aesthetic approach to reflect this shift in the body politic, theatre practitioners turned to *The Theatre and its*

Double as a source of inspiration. In 1958, the first English translation became available and, from that moment onwards, Artaud's influence over theatre practice was assured. Artaud's polemic writing offered the artists of this generation so much more than previous theatre-revolutionaries could. His revolt was an all-consuming one that aimed to destroy the structures of Western civilisation both socially and personally, which much outflanked the old-fashioned Marxism of Bertolt Brecht or Erwin Piscator.

It is somewhat misleading to suggest that, thanks to the sociopolitical developments of the 1960s, it is now fully possible to realise the Theatre of Cruelty. Rather, practitioners have used Artaud's writing as a starting block for their own aesthetic projects, expanding the boundaries of performance to incorporate Artaudian ideas into the everyday vocabulary of theatre practice. However, contemporary practitioners experimenting with the Theatre of Cruelty have found it difficult to identify a tangible starting point in Artaud's praxis, as he specified no concrete training technique. Additionally, it would be futile for practitioners to recreate any of his mostly failed performance projects because their idiosyncrasies reveal little about the fundamentals of Artaudian acting. In truth, Artaud never considered it important to pursue this angle, instead relying on his followers to establish the essential techniques. After the humiliating collapse of *The Cenci*, Artaud felt compelled to write a technical essay to counter suggestions that his theories were impracticable. The result was 'An Affective Athleticism', collected in *The Theatre and its Double*, but the essay only half delivers its promise, imparting merely a few disparate clues. Frustratingly, he claims:

> I wanted to restrict myself to examples bearing on the few fertile principles comprising the material of this technical essay. Others, if they have time, can draw up the complete structure of the method.
>
> (*CW4*, p.105)

However, such disciples to the Theatre of Cruelty did not materialise until a decade after his death.

A brief review of significant post-1960 theatre practitioners demonstrates the extent to which Artaud's ideas have reverberated in contemporary practice. In Poland, Jerzy Grotowski's Poor Theatre employed Artaud's writing as a stimulus with which to rethink the aesthetics of theatre performance. He appreciated Artaud's attitude towards the physical and spiritual life of the performer and continued Artaud's investigation of how inner impulses can be given external expression through the body. Like Artaud, Grotowski sought a pure, almost metaphysical, approach to training and performing, aiming to remove the obstacles between the performer's physical and psychic self. Through his training programme, the performer becomes an athlete, mastering complete control over their psychophysical abilities and rekindling a spiritual relationship with the spectator.

In America, the Living Theatre, run by Julian Beck and Judith Malina, was developing guerrilla performances that rejected the conventional theatre's dependence upon fiction. Instead, their new theatre promoted the radical political and aesthetic views of the company. Their masterpiece, *Paradise Now,* took the form of a long ritual that aimed to impact spiritually and metaphysically upon the audience, urging them to recognise and free themselves from state control. As a consequence of partaking in the production, Beck and Malina hoped to instigate a personal revolution within each spectator that would ultimately trigger a wider social revolution in their real lives. In the mid 1960s, Joseph Chaikin (an actor from the Living Theatre) formed the Open Theatre to investigate the suspicious relationship between the performer and the character. Promoting collective creation and a radical break from realism, Chaikin drew upon Grotowski's psychophysical exercises as a method of liberating the performer from their restrictive training in character-based naturalism. Similarly, the director Richard Schechner collapsed the boundaries between the performer's life and art. The result was an unpredictable and primal presentation where performers revealed their personal vulnerabilities and the tensions in the group dynamic became visible in each performance.

In England, Peter Brook and Charles Marowitz undertook *The Theatre of Cruelty Season* (1964) at the Royal Shakespeare Company, aiming to explore ways in which Artaud's ideas could be used to find new forms of expression and retrain the performer. The result was a showing of 'works in progress' made up of improvisations and sketches, one of which was the premier of Artaud's *The Spurt of Blood* (some four decades after it was written). Although the experiment was met with mixed reviews, the Artaudian ideas developed by Brook and Marowitz have informed many of Brook's subsequent productions – most notably his production of Peter Weiss' *Marat-Sade*. As J.C. Trewin's account from the time confirms, the asylum around which this play revolves was depicted through "a frightening variety of Artaudian shocks, everything from hallucinations, paroxysms, executions, and whippings, to cries and moans, an infinity of sound variations, and a startling use of make-up." The actors (most of whom were taken from *The Theatre of Cruelty Season*) were required to search for the madmen and madwomen inside themselves, rather than 'represent' madness on stage.

As this narrow review of Artaud's influence suggests, the Theatre of Cruelty does not exist per se, but rather its influence has unlocked new possibilities for modern-day practitioners. Furthermore, many of these practitioners have commented in one way or another that it is impossible to fully realise a Theatre of Cruelty and that its potency is as a source of poetic inspiration and a set of impossible questions. It is a theatre of process rather than product. In the following workshops, we will examine the shreds of guidance offered to us by Artaud and then examine how his followers have responded to his challenges in order to identify workable Artaudian techniques.

WORKSHOP 1: *Finding a New Theatrical Vocabulary*

The longevity of Artaud's influence is closely linked to his heresy. Practitioners discovering his writing for the first time have been enthused by the artistic possibilities that arise from the proposed destruction of drama's literary history. Artaud encourages his readers to 'wipe the slate clean' and question the fundamental ideas underpinning conventional theatre. In this workshop, we shall review some of the Artaudian techniques developed by practitioners to give physical and vocal expression to the thought before the word. Adapted from Joseph Chaikin's work, this first exercise places the verbal and physical life of a character in disharmony, demonstrating Artaud's view that theatre becomes infinitely more engaging once it escapes its reliance upon verbal language.

Exercise One: **'Opposites'**

1 Working individually, participants find a physical expression of an extreme emotion or feeling. Whilst the choice of stimulus is at the discretion of the participant, encourage them to move away from realism and discover more abstract physical gestures. The result may be a physical movement that travels across the space, can be developed standing, or performed on the floor.

2 Once developed, instruct the participants to evolve this into four or five sequential movements that can be repeated in a continual loop, stretching each physical gesture to its extreme.

3 Each participant must now overlay a vocal 'score' to their sequence that contradicts their physicality. For example, if one performer is happily sauntering across the space, they may decide to add a series of short horrific screams. Similarly, if another is writhing in agony on the floor, then they could whistle a happy tune.

4 Perform each sequence to the group and discuss the effect of separating the vocal and physical in performance. What happens when realism is removed?

Chaikin's work concentrated on the Artaudian concept that the performer's presence is more important than characterisation. He distinguished between the "inside" and "outside" of a performer, a view borrowed from the crux of Artaud's 'An Affective Athleticism'. In this essay, Artaud proposed the removal of the boundary between the inner and outer self, connecting the performer's metaphysical and physical being. Artaud's actor training forms the basis of a method aimed at reversing the limiting effects of Western psychology upon the performer. They must discipline themselves to enable physical gestures to emerge directly from their subconscious, therefore bypassing their rational mind and transgressing the boundary between the inner and outer self. In short, Artaud believed that theatre could achieve that which his poetry and prose could not accomplish – the articulation of the thought before the word. There is little evidence to suggest that Artaud actualised this idea during his own artistic career but, as the following two exercises demonstrate, his concept has followed through into contemporary theatre practice. Both exercises have been adapted from a Mladen Materic workshop and should be explored together. The first exercise examines what Artaud means by an "impulsive gesture" that is indescribable by speech, and the second develops these into movement sequences.

Exercise Two: 'Materic's Impulse Game'

1   Very simply, a tennis ball is thrown across a circle from participant to participant, each slightly accentuating the way in which they catch, aim and throw the ball. Try varying this simple game by rotating the circle, miming the ball, moving around the space or with multiple balls. Briefly discuss how participants knew that the ball was going to be thrown to them. What physical signals or impulses were they noticing?

2   Now introduce a variation. Each participant must 'trick' the person they are going to throw the ball to by directing their impulse elsewhere in the circle. For example, you might look at one person across the circle and direct your body language towards them, but just as the ball leaves your hand, you throw to someone entirely different. Every time the ball is dropped, that person is out. The game is played until only one performer remains.

3   Discuss the difference between the two versions of the game and identify why one was harder than the other.

Exercise Three: 'Impulsive Gesture'

For this exercise to be effective, the participants must be fully warmed up and at ease with each other.

1   Each participant must lay on their back with their eyes closed. They should become aware of their own bodies, sense their weight upon the studio floor, feel their chest cavities expanding and contracting, and feel the blood pumping around their body.

2   Instruct the performers to make any movement they like, follow it through and see where it takes them. Try not to 'decide' on a movement, but instead try to 'taste' it. Let it come from the body, not the mind. Once that movement has come to its natural end, make another and follow that one through. The trick is to spend a lot of time on this part of the exercise so that the participants become sensitive to the subtle movements within their own bodies. Once they are accustomed, try it from a sitting position, then kneeling and finally standing.

3   Each participant selects the starting position they most favour and makes a single movement. Each move is an impulse that generates another in the body. For example, movement in the shoulder may stretch the spine – which in turn begins a rotation in the hips – which brings one leg into a crouching position – which curves the spine into a foetal shape and so on. Each action should merge seamlessly and simultaneously with the next until the participant's body is in a continual state of flux.

4   This exercise can be developed for advanced groups. Working in pairs (A and B), stand facing each other and start moving in flux responding to both their own and their partner's movements. It is sometimes useful to start with an exchange of movement (A,B,A,B) and then move into flux.

5   Discuss how it felt making the movements and how the participants relied on an impulse moving from one part of their body to the next rather than making a 'conscious' decision.

The development of subconscious organic movements that are kinaesthetically amplified is clearly an Artaudian concept, here, formalised by Materic. Artaud also demanded that a similar organic approach be applied to the voice. In *To Have Done with the Judgement of God* Artaud performs a series of soundscapes, employing glossolalia as a performance technique. Allen S. Weiss is among the few critics who have successfully unravelled Artaud's glossolalia and screams to reveal their texture and complexity. In his following definition we can again see how Artaud attempted to bypass his conscious mind:

> Glossolalia is a type of speech or babble ... It is the manifestation of language at the level of its pure materiality, the realm of pure sound ... As such, the relation between sound and meaning breaks down through the glossolalic utterance...

Artaud pushes language to its limits, attempting to generate speech that expresses his inner thought before its impulse is lost during the translation into words. Reflecting similar developments in his poetry, Artaud's glossolalia transcends conventional meaning and takes on the tone of an incantation. One of the scripted sections of glossolalia in *To Have Done with the Judgement of God* reads: "o reche modo / to edire / di za / tau dari / do padera coco." When read aloud as intended, the poetic nature of this text is unmistakable, employing hard consonant sounds and rhythmic similarities between the invented words (for example: "modo ... coco" or "to edire ... tau dari"). It is the sonic vibrancy of these sounds that carries Artaud's glossolalia evoking primitive rituals and speaking in tongues. Although Materic's above exercise is only a physical manifestation of this process, it is possible for the workshop participants to add a vocal dimension in the latter stages with some interesting results. However, the following exercise, taken from Beck and Malina's *Mysteries and the Smaller Pieces*, makes an interesting link between Artaud's glossolalia and ritual. Originally, the exercise was developed by Chaikin and the Open Theatre, but was borrowed by the Living Theatre in 1964 and incorporated into their production.

Exercise Four: 'Glossolalia: Bypassing Rationalisation'

1   The participants form two lines on either side of the space, facing each other. Someone improvises a movement and a sound which they direct towards someone opposite. The recipient of the movement and sound must react to its impulse, transform it and

direct it towards someone opposite. And so the game continues. If played seriously for a long time, the movements organically change the vocalisations and remove the need for rationalisation. Continue until the full range of sounds and actions have been explored.

2   Once fully accomplished, you could try varying the 'theme' of the exercise. Review what Artaud writes about the plague and use the exercise to vocalise the agonies of a plague-infected body.

3   Review and discuss. Were the sounds generated by the rational part of the mind – if not, where were they generated? How could this ritual be developed?

For Artaud, the body must both 'breathe hieroglyphs' and become a 'physical hieroglyph', giving the thought before the word a concrete manifestation in the stage space. This new theatrical language was to be articulated through primal rituals, designed to appeal directly to the subconscious of the spectator and destabilise their trust in conventional language, rationality and psychology.

WORKSHOP 2:   *Ritual and Cruelty*

Let us first identify what we mean by 'ritual'. The term seems much underused considering that every aspect of our daily routine operates through it, informing our social activities and interactions. Therefore, ritual extends beyond its familiar religious context because our customs, traditions and habits underpin every action we undertake (both formal and personal). Artaud identified these forces at work in everyday life and regarded the theatre as an ideal place to harness their power. Through theatre, Artaud believed that he could force individuals to viscerally experience the natural, primitive and animalistic rituals with which Western living has lost all contact. Although never explicit about this idea, Artaud did differentiate between primitive rituals and those that have been instituted by Western civilisation. The Artaudian performer must be 'cruel' to both the self and the audience by exposing and rejecting banal civilised rituals and intensifying primitive ones. This idea formed the aesthetic principle behind many post-1960 theatre companies where it was considered essential for performers to detect and subvert 'respectable' Western rituals. In particular, Chaikin trained his performers to find the taboo (or 'cruelty' in Artaudian terms) of any given situation. The following exercise is taken from one of the Open Theatre's improvisations.

Exercise One: 'The Taboo'

1 A small group pick a banal, everyday social situation within which they can improvise. Examples may include a meal in a restaurant, a long distance train journey or hosting a party for business clients. The director secretly selects one participant to perform the taboo.

2 The improvisation begins. Waiting for the best opportunity, the secretly chosen participant must attempt to overstep the boundaries of the social situation they are in. Explain that the taboo must emerge from the scenario naturally rather than be outlandishly shocking. For example, in a very formal situation, the taboo might be to reveal something deeply personal, or a tired businessman may lay his head upon the lap of a colleague; all logical scenarios, but unacceptable in their specific social contexts.

3 Review and discuss the rituals at work in everyday social situations and the consequent effect when they were undermined.

Rituals dictate our social behaviour and it is through the performance of these rituals that Western civilisation exerts its control over the masses. By exposing and eliminating Western counterfeit rituals, Artaud believed that the Theatre of Cruelty could create a spiritual connection between the spectator, the performer and metaphysical truth. Therefore, both the performer and the spectator become equal components in the performance, their presence transforming the action and the theatre space around them. It becomes a "total theatre" where the entire event becomes one overarching hieroglyph within which every object, performer and spectator contribute to the overall *mise-en-scène*.

Evidently, this impacts heavily upon the role of the performer, reducing their significance and rethinking their function in the theatrical event. This idea was explored in the process of *The Theatre of Cruelty Season* at the RSC. In searching for ways to overcome their actors' reliance upon psychological naturalism, Brook and Marowitz created rituals with the group where sounds and rhythms were "redefined in exact, physical terms". For the following exercise,

I have adapted and extended Marowitz's rehearsal notes from this seminal project.

Exercise Two: 'Introduction to Sounds'

1 The group is presented with a pile of random objects – broom handles, cardboard boxes, metal pipes, tins, crates, etc. They are instructed to find a musical instrument from the objects and explore the range of sounds it can 'play'.

2 The group stands in a circle and someone plays out a rhythm. One by one, the rest of the group joins in to create a whole group percussion piece. Without an elected leader to conduct them, the group must craft the sound, changing the tempo, the intensity and the combinations of instruments. Allow time for the group to explore this in depth, as the longer the exercise, the more interesting the results.

3 Give the group a scenario to musically score. If they are having trouble with this idea, start with an intelligible scenario like an army of mercenaries marching into the distance, but then start to push their creativity. Narratives could include a riot erupting in the street which is then dispersed by police, or a lone boatman falling overboard in a storm.

4 Participants must now introduce physical movements and vocal sounds which extend from their instruments. Develop these movements into walks so that each performer can travel around the space and play. Remember, a thudding bass instrument would move differently to an alto one. Once developed, take the instruments away from each participant instructing them to continue with their vocal and physical work.

5 Again, the group is instructed to craft their soundscape by changing tempo, intensity and instrument combinations.

6 Finish and discuss the effects of taking part in this long sound ritual. How did the group make performance decisions? What was the effect of the ritual upon the body, the voice and the individual/group consciousness? Could the sounds communicate feelings and ideas?

Artaud's theatrical rituals appeal to the primitive self, granting purpose to the participants. They engulf the performer and the spectator in a vortex, consuming the individual and forming a group consciousness. The euphoria of partaking in such a ritual ushers the participant into new territory, transcending the limits prescribed by Western civilisation – to surpass oneself (in Grotowski's terms).

To exemplify the power of ritual, I have adapted a Schechner exercise in which the company performed a sacrifice, doubling up as a revenge act upon an actor responsible for an accident the previous day. Although fierce and primitive, the ritual had redemptive powers in the group dynamic. As Schechner described it, "A certain justice had been done for the night before."

Exercise Three: 'The Sacrifice Ritual'

This exercise can have a profound effect on individuals in a group and must only be attempted with mature performers who are truly at ease with one another.

1 Explain that when the director rings a bell, someone in the room must be sacrificed for the well-being of the whole village. Without discussion, the group must turn on one of their own and dance and play them to death. Only once the chosen 'victim' feels suitably overwhelmed by the entire group (which may take several minutes) can they act out their death.

2 Distribute the instruments from Exercise Two and ask the performers to begin playing in small groups. They must play with one group for a minute or so, and then move on to another, introducing paralinguistic sounds into their rhythms. After a while, ring the bell and study how the group dynamic shifts. How is the 'victim' chosen? How are they danced and played to death?

3 Once the ritual is complete, announce that everyone must now partake in the "magic of life" ritual and revive the 'victim's' limp body. The whole group must move the body to the most holy place in the studio and begin the magic ritual without discussion. Only once the 'victim' feels fully loved by the group, can they awake.

4 Discuss the impact of the ritual upon the group and upon the 'victim'. It is essential to debrief this exercise fully and in positive terms.

This exercise is powerful because it transgresses the boundary between the aesthetic and personal lives of the participants. Although the group is undertaking a fictional scenario, the choice of victim and the method of sacrifice forces the participants to draw upon the real group dynamic. For Schechner, this merging of art and life through ritual is at the heart of Artaud's concept of "the double". Reflecting upon 'The Sacrifice Ritual', he wrote:

> The exercise truly took on the form of a theatrical ritual, with all the mystery that implies. It was real and unreal, authentic and acted out. No one was dying, but two people were dying; there was no village, but there was one all the same. The "double" that Artaud speaks of so knowingly in relation to the theatre was there.

Artaud's theatrical ritual extends beyond the aesthetic boundaries of conventional theatre and 'cruelly' exposes the vulnerabilities of the participants. In this sense, the Theatre of Cruelty becomes a theatrical ceremony which gives redemption and meaning to the lives of its participants.

WORKSHOP 3: *The Performer and Audience Relationship*

Artaud wanted to remove the division between the auditorium and the stage, allowing the action to spread into every corner of the space. He believed that the audience had been disempowered by the very architecture of traditional theatres, and that realism had disqualified the audience altogether, reducing them to an invisible, inanimate fourth wall. Artaud's counteraction was to hurl his audience into the very centre of the action where "Direct contact will be established between the audience and the show, between actors and audience ..." He envisaged an escape from traditional theatre spaces and a move into unrestricted hangers and barns. The audience, seated in the centre on swivelling chairs, could watch the action take place on the multilevel platforms that surround them, the action organically unfolding from one side of the space to the other. Action, image and sound would simultaneously occur from all directions, allowing the audience to select their own perspective and make their own connections between the production's elements. However, Artaud did specify a performance area that could be used to build climaxes by concentrating the action into one central place. In effect, Artaud advocated a return to theatre's origins, incorporating the spectator at the heart of the ritual rather than excluding them altogether. Brook's own methodology draws upon this idea, claiming that "We have lost all sense of ritual and ceremony", and that we, "clap our hands mechanically because we do not know what else to do …" Many years after Artaud's death, Schechner coined the term "environmental theatre" to describe the cohabitation of actor and spectator in the theatre space, arguing that the architecture of the venue manipulates and sculpts the performance. To explore this idea, I have expanded an exercise used by Schechner when rehearsing the Performance Group.

Exercise One: 'Habitats'

1   Without using speech to communicate, the group must landscape the rehearsal space by first selecting an area in the room which they feel personally drawn towards. They must build a habitat for themselves that in some way reflects their personality from any materials to hand – chairs, tables, mats, boxes, rostra, clothes, bags, etc. Where one may erect a high-up fortress, another may build a small burrow.

2   Instruct each individual to develop a ritual to perform upon entering their habitat and an animalistic way of scaring off intruders. Once in role, they must remain focused throughout the improvisation and protect their habitat at all costs. They can stray from their enclosures, but must remain close enough to protect them. Whenever they return, they must perform their ritual.

3   Invite a small audience into the space to explore the landscape. The performers must react to the outsiders in role. The more confident ones may occasionally allow individuals near enough to interact, whilst others may do everything within their power to warn them off.

4   Reflect upon the exercise in terms of how the landscape has been constructed (what does it say about the group consciousness?) and how the presence of the audience changed the atmosphere and dynamic of the space.

The idea of 'opening up the space' is clearly borrowed from Artaud's conception of a total theatre where every element contributes to the overall hieroglyph and where the spectator becomes an active ingredient in the performance. The emphasis upon ritual is again evident in this idea; that there is a non-verbal 'contract' between the audience and performer, the rules of which govern the conduct of any interaction. The lives of the spectators and performers connect through a joint ritual that creates an exhilarating 'opening up' of consciousness. This idea became embedded in the radical art practices of the 1960s and 1970s. Notably, performance artist Gina Pane emphasised this unspoken contract in her 1971 performance, *Nourriture, Actualités télévisées, feu*. She ritualised the social transaction that lies at the heart of the theatrical event by demanding that her audience deposit two per cent of their annual salary into a metal chest before being admitted. I have drawn upon this idea in the next exercise, amalgamating it with two of Marowitz's rehearsal activities, to practically explore the audience-performer contract.

Exercise Two: 'Gifts'

1 Arrange to meet five participants before a group rehearsal. They must select a real-life embarrassing moment or story to reveal to the group and develop it into an improvised two-minute monologue.

2 Once rehearsed, produce five objects which each make a noise (a whistle, a chime, a bell and so on). The whistle will cue performer one, the chime performer two and so forth. The director will sound any of the five objects at random intervals, however, three rules must be observed: 1) Only one participant can perform their monologue at any given moment. Therefore, a speaker must cut out mid-syllable if another performer is cued. 2) When they hear their sound again, they must continue their story from the exact point they left off. 3) When a performer reaches the end of their monologue, they must cue another by tapping their shoulder, retrieve their sound object and exit the space. Run the whole exercise until the space is empty.

3 When the rest of the group arrive, ask them to wait outside. Prepare the performers to run the exercise and place the objects on the floor around them. Greet the audience and inform them that they,

"may interact with the performers by using the objects surrounding them". Before they can enter the space, each audience member must deposit an item of personal value in a box. The box is placed between the performers in full view of the spectators during the performance. Allow the audience to position themselves in relation to the performance area and wait for them to make the first sound – triggering the first monologue. The performance continues until all five performers have left the space. The audience is then instructed to take their personal belongings from the box and depart.

4   Reflect and discuss the nature of the audience/performer contract and the effect of audience interaction. Interrogate the audience about their reactions.

The removal of aesthetic distance produces an inclusive theatrical experience. Artaud hoped that an encounter with the Theatre of Cruelty would have a lasting effect upon the spectator and render them more receptive to metaphysical experiences. Whilst this may seem like naive idealism on Artaud's behalf, it is the purity of his theatrical vision that has unlocked new aesthetic possibilities in today's theatre. However, this purity is compromised by the play text, a stubborn literary form that regulates and steers a performance to a predetermined outcome. Artaud's theatre is fluid, continually reacting to the presence of the spectator, and consequently, the pre-set inflexible narrative of conventional theatre is outmoded. Thus, Artaud called for a reconsideration of the role of the author and a re-evaluation of theatre's literary history.

WORKSHOP 4: *Approaching Text*

Considering Artaud's attitude towards written text, it is peculiar that he also considered producing pre-existing plays for the Theatre of Cruelty. His uncompromising disdain towards conventional playwriting is evident throughout his texts and is deeply ingrained into his artistic approach. His clipped definition states:

> Dialogue – something written and spoken – does not specifically belong to the stage but to books.
>
> (*CW4*, p.25)

Artaud's condemnation of celebrated playwrights is also a reflection of this crucial idea, holding Shakespeare and his followers responsible for theatre's literary stagnation. However, Artaud did not set out to completely eliminate the play text, but rather 'dethrone' it and reduce its importance. As discussed in Chapter 4, Artaud identified the scenario (rather than the full-length manuscript) as the superior format through which to present theatrical ideas in written form because it provided a framework for the process rather than a blueprint for the final product. The maxim 'process, not product' characterises Artaud's adaptation of pre-existing text, using the dialogue as a stimulus for practical exploration. This informed Schechner's approach to Euripides' *The Bacchae,* where the conventional structures of the play were rejected in favour of a series of improvisations based around the thematic elements of the text. The following improvisation is adapted from one used during this production.

Exercise One: 'The Bacchae'

1   Look at the start of the play: Dionysus, God of wine, has returned to Thebes to punish his followers for no longer worshipping him. It is the new King, Pentheus, who has banned Dionysian worship, suspecting that the rites are simply a cheap justification for lewd and depraved behaviour, undermining the moral laws of Thebes. Pentheus' first speech explores this. Ask every participant to select lines that they feel sum up why the rites were banned or lines which present Dionysus in a negative light. Learn them as quickly as possible and in any order.

2   Select one performer to experience Dionysus' growing frustration. Everyone else must find a place in the room from which they can deliver their selected lines. Dionysus' motivation is to silence the multiple voices of Pentheus by placing his hand over their mouths. When silenced for the first time, they must count to fifty and begin again, the second time they count to forty, then thirty and so on, until they cannot be silenced for more than a few seconds. Once Dionysus reaches the point of near exhaustion, he must collapse in the centre of the room and allow the voices to overpower him.

3 Run the improvisation/game and discuss its effects upon the performers, the protagonist and an audience. Was it successful in communicating the theme of the scene? How could it be adjusted to increase Dionysus' frustration? Agree any changes and try again.

The author's intentions are completely abandoned and a new 'life' in the text is found, one which focuses upon the themes behind the narrative. Artaud suggested a number of suitable plays that could be adapted for his theatre, giving considerable thought to John Ford's *'Tis Pity She's a Whore*. His account of the suitable elements of this play ignores the narrative structure altogether and focuses on the thematic content, notably the incest between Annabella and Giovanni, a crime of lust that ignores society's moral boundaries. For Artaud, the conventions of playwriting obscure the deeper, more appealing themes of the play. In considering why Sophocles' *Oedipus Rex* no longer appeals to the masses, when the play is brimming with incest, plague and fate, he notes that these universal themes are "clothed in language which has lost any contact with today's crude, epileptic rhythm". Cutting to the core of a text in order to emphasise its thematic subtext encapsulates the Artaudian approach to pre-existing plays, and licensed post-1960 practitioners to discover the visceral nuance behind the words. During *The Theatre of Cruelty Season*, Brook and Marowitz used this technique in their presentation of *Hamlet*, with the following Artaudian intention:

> It's an attempt to open up the play from inside – to redistribute all its elements, and try to see if one can present the play free from conventional narrative and still give the essence of what it's about.[1]

This approach can be taken with many texts and, through workshop, performers can invent and experiment with an array of improvisations that fracture and redistribute text in similar ways to Schechner's exercise for *The Bacchae*.

It seems curious that whilst Artaud was dismantling existing plays to make them suitable for his theatre, he was also writing his own plays in a conventional manner. The only reasonable justification for this inconsistency is to note that Roger Blin's blocking diagrams for the 1935 production of *The Cenci* reveal that the physical stage action was vastly more complex than the manuscript itself suggests.[2] However, the play's conventionality is inescapable. Finding alternative methods with which to approach Artaud's own texts formed part of Brook and Marowitz's work, and it is from their experiment that I have taken the following exercise.

Exercise Two: 'The Spurt of Blood'

1 First, read Artaud's *The Spurt of Blood* as a group (it is very brief!) and divide the text into short sections. Each group of four must select a different section with which to work.

2 Using the extract as a stimulus, each group must devise a soundscape of screams, sighs and breathing patterns to communicate the action. Each sound must follow either the rhythm of the speech or the action of the stage directions, unlocking the 'textures' of the text.

3 Get the groups to mix up and form a large circle. Practise the sections aloud, projecting the voice across the room. Through rehearsal, link the sections smoothly, add extra sounds or random snippets from the text and craft the overall dynamic of the piece.

4 Either invite a tiny audience to sit in the centre of the circle or take it in turns to listen. Turn the lights out and perform the soundscape.

5 Finally, review and discuss which elements of the play were evident in your performance. How does this exercise link with the other workshops in this chapter?

Artaud's attitude towards the play text is a reflection of his core principles. Conventional theatre (and the naturalism movement) is concerned with mimesis, materially copying reality in a spiritless manner. Artaud's theatre is also concerned with reality, but aims to transform and extend it, viscerally intensifying the spectator's experience rather than excluding them from the event. Thus, the play text must also be transformed and extended, shattering its mimetic surface and releasing the metaphysical power beneath.

*   *   *

This chapter set out to question the practicability of Artaud's theatre practice. Is it now sufficient to suggest that the directors detailed in this chapter have achieved that which Artaud could not? Although the creative endeavours of Artaud's followers have drawn upon his ideas in an innovative and provoking way, their practice cannot be labelled with the 'Theatre of Cruelty' tag. Indeed, the Living Theatre were given pre-publish access to the first English translation of *The Theatre and its Double* and were enthused by the parallels between their work, but were already engaged in their own aesthetic direction. In his book on the Living Theatre, Pierre Biner writes:

> As it turned out, the Living Theatre was to stay content to follow its natural inclinations and to make do without Artaud, although the discovery of Artaud's work was an invaluable stimulus, confirmation, and encouragement to them.

Each of the practitioners discussed in this chapter, in their own way, have explored only part of the overall terrain, selecting ideas of importance for their own artistic projects. Consequently, I have not been able to explicate the Theatre of Cruelty per se, but have been able to explore Artaud's practical influence upon contemporary theatre.

Does this therefore mean that the Theatre of Cruelty is an impossible concept? This is a complex question to answer accurately because Artaud's theatre can only exist after an extreme social upheaval: let us not forget that his proposal, and the rhetoric that accompanied it, demanded a complete 'overthrow' of present-day theatre rather than a 'development' of it. In the notes he prepared for his final public appearance, *A Tête-à-Tête with Antonin Artaud,* he wrote:

> The Theatre of Cruelty was never realized because its very existence presupposes the disappearance of the basis of public life which is called Society.
>
> *(AT,* p.202)

Therefore, semantically, when Artaud wrote about his Theatre of Cruelty, he was not referring to 'theatre' as is currently conceived at all, but to a new, untested social practice that was to replace it. Furthermore, Artaud's theatre was a means to an end; namely, to correct the errors of Western civilisation and to bring the masses into contact with their metaphysical selves – their doubles. In this sense, the Theatre of Cruelty is, in fact, a spiritual concept, a form which transcends the aesthetic boundaries of performance and can be more correctly defined as a social and artistic 'approach'. Artaud did not confine this approach to the realms of theatre, but also applied it to a variety of other art forms including poetry, radio, drawing, public lecture and cinema, in an attempt to disrupt the social rituals of the masses. It is therefore impossible to assess the success or failure of the Theatre of Cruelty in isolation from its accompanying revolution. Accordingly, Artaud's passion for theatre is hindered by the questions he asks: Is theatre socially relevant? Is there any relationship between performance and text? Why persist with theatre at all?

Notes

[1]   Here, Marowitz and Brook are in interview with Simon Trussler for the February 1964 edition of *Plays and Players*. This citation is taken from its reprint in Williams' *Peter Brook: A Theatrical Casebook* (p.29).

[2]   Blin's blocking diagrams were included in 'Antonin Artaud's *Les Cenci*', *The Drama Review* (June 1972, Vol. 16, No. 2). Please see the bibliography for more details.

Conclusion

"From one body to another."

In the closing pages of this book, I would like to return to the central question that has surfaced throughout my exploration of the link between Artaud's theory and practice – did Artaud fail? This question has many angles, and therefore, we must first clarify it. If the question is asking whether Artaud failed to realise his theatre proposals in his own lifetime, then the answer must be a resolute 'yes'. As Chapter Four concludes, his productions were flawed by material circumstances and, in part, his inability to communicate his ideas with lucidity. Whilst this case against Artaud is highly convincing, the strength of his posthumous influence offers a countercharge. Here, Artaud's failure to stage the Theatre of Cruelty himself is offset by the work of his followers who have used his theories as a basis for their own practice. It is through *their* work that Artaud has been able to exert his influence over contemporary theatre, and in this sense, he did (posthumously) achieve his aims. However, this 'Artaudian renaissance' illuminates only the influence of the Theatre of Cruelty, not its practicability. As discussed elsewhere, Artaud proposed a theatre of process, rather than product. Therefore, there is validity in the argument that the success or failure of the Theatre of Cruelty should not be based upon works like *The Spurt of Blood*, *The Philosopher's Stone*, *The Conquest of Mexico*, *The Cenci* or *To Have Done with the Judgement of God*.

The consideration of Artaud's success or failure becomes more interesting once we move beyond a literal response to the question and incorporate his philosophic aims into the debate. Certainly, there is little evidence to suggest that he managed to bring his audience into contact with their metaphysical doubles or expose them to the

Gnostic metaphysical truths of the universe. However, Artaud did attempt to project his own body into the metaphysical realm. He rethought his body as a non-material substance, described as a "body without organs" in *To Have Done with the Judgement of God,* and his writing became a form of escape from the pain of his diseased body, an attempt to live without flesh and an attempt to achieve immortality. Poetically, there is a sense that Artaud has managed to live on through his writing – certainly, his presence has been strongly felt since his death in 1948. Furthermore, the visceral tone of Artaud's writing derives from his attempts to project his essence, his pain and his presence into every word. Like Nietzsche, Artaud is convinced that physical existence is an aesthetic illusion, and therefore, his life-essence can live on in his art. As we have discovered earlier in this book, his name emerges from the text of 'Theatre and the Plague', Count Cenci embodies Artaud's own moral stance and recites passages from his essays, and the screams in *To Have Done with the Judgement of God* project Artaud's pain across the airwaves.

Artaud is our contemporary precisely because we cannot escape his body, his essence or the actuality of his life. In this way, Artaud himself becomes the 'subject' of his writing, lurking in the subtext where no distinction can be drawn between his life and his art. In one of his last poems, entitled 'Who Am I?', Artaud has accepted his forthcoming physical death from which he believes a more permanent body will arise – one that cannot be forgotten:

> I am Antonin Artaud
> and I proclaim it ...
> you'll see my real body
> shatter
> and reassemble ...
> a new body
> in which you will never be able
> to forget me.

(AT, p.234)

Bibliography

Texts by Artaud:

Of the 25 volumes of Artaud's *Collected Works* published in France, only four English translations are in print. I have used the following abbreviations throughout the book: *CW1-4* refers to the four translations of *Collected Works*, *AT* refers to *Artaud on Theatre*, and *WI* refers to quotations from *Wireless Imagination: Sound, Radio, and the Avant-Garde*. For ease of reference, I have indicated which volumes contain the significant texts referred to in this study.

Antonin Artaud, *Collected Works: Volume One* (Calder and Boyars: London, 1968), translated by Victor Corti. Includes *Correspondence with Jacques Rivière*, *The Spurt of Blood*, *Writing is all Trash*, and his open letters for the surrealists.

Antonin Artaud, *Collected Works: Volume Two* (Calder and Boyars: London, 1971), translated by Victor Corti. Includes *The Philosopher's Stone*.

Antonin Artaud, *Collected Works: Volume Three* (Calder and Boyars: London, 1972), translated by Alastair Hamilton. Includes interviews and letters.

Antonin Artaud, *Collected Works: Volume Four* (Calder and Boyars: London, 1974), translated by Victor Corti. Includes *The Theatre and its Double* and *The Cenci*.

Claude Schumacher and Brian Singleton (eds.), *Artaud on Theatre* (Methuen Drama: London, 2001). Contains valuable key texts not included in *Collected Works* including *The Conquest of Mexico*, *Theatre and the Gods*, and a selection of letters and articles surrounding *To Have Done with the Judgement of God* and *The Cenci*.

Douglas Kahn and Gregory Whitehead (eds.), *Wireless Imagination: Sound, Radio, and the Avant-Garde* (MIT Press: Massachusetts, 1994). Contains *To Have Done with the Judgement of God*, translated in full by Clayton Eshleman, accompanied by Allen S. Weiss' insightful essay 'Radio, Death, and the Devil'.

Books and biographies on Artaud used in this study include:

Stephen Barber, *Antonin Artaud: Blows and Bombs* (Faber and Faber: London, 1993). The most conscientious Artaud biography, balancing his remarkable life with critical insight. For an astute commentary on Artaud's audio recordings, I recommend Barber's *The Screaming Body* (Creation Books: London, 1999).

Albert Bermel, *Artaud's Theatre of Cruelty* (Taplinger Publishing: New York, 1977). A useful, wide-ranging study, but is now dated. Much more useful is Bermel's chapter on *The Spurt of Blood* in *Contradictory Characters* (E.P. Dutton and Co: New York, 1973).

Robert Brustein, *The Theatre of Revolt: An Approach to the Modern Drama* (Ivan R. Dee: Chicago, 1991). Contains valuable accounts of Artaud's influence over modern theatre, specifically over the writing of Jean Genet.

Martin Esslin, *Artaud* (William Collins Sons & Co: Glasgow, 1976). This book opened new directions in the study of Artaud by contextualising his art with his life. Wide ranging and critically astute.

Edward Scheer (ed.), *Antonin Artaud: A Critical Reader* (Routledge: London, 2004). This book collects the key texts that have furthered the academic study of Artaud. As such, this book is indispensable to any Artaud enthusiast. The essays I have used in this monograph include 'Artaud, Defecation and Birth' by Leo Bersani, 'The Theatre of Cruelty and the Closure of Representation' and 'To Unsense the Subjectile' by Jacques Derrida, 'The Plague and its Powers in Artaudian Theatre' by Jane Goodall, 'He Wasn't Entirely Himself' by Jerzy Grotowski, 'The Subject in Process' by Julia Kristeva and 'Approaching Artaud' by Susan Sontag.

Journal articles used in this study include:

'Antonin Artaud's *Les Cenci*', *The Drama Review* (June 1972, Vol. 16, No. 2). A dossier of documents pertinent to the 1935 production of *The Cenci*. Importantly, extracts from Roger Blin's production notebook are reproduced with diagrams.

Rustom Bharucha, 'Eclecticism, Oriental Theater and Artaud', *Theater* (Summer 1978, Vol. 9, No. 3). An informed account of Artaud and Oriental performance.

Rodolphe Gasché, 'Self-Engendering as a Verbal Body', *Modern Language Notes* (May 1978, Vol 93, No. 4). A skilful deconstruction of Artaud's writing.

Martin Harries, 'Forgetting Lot's Wife: Artaud, Spectatorship, and Catastrophe', *The Yale Journal of Criticism* (Spring 1998, Vol 11, No. 1).

Nicola Savarese, '1931: Antonin Artaud Sees Balinese Theatre at the Paris Colonial Exposition', *The Drama Review* (Fall 2001, Vol. 45, No. 3), translated by Richard Fowler. A historical account of the event that triggered the Theatre of Cruelty.

Other works referred to in this study:

Pierre Biner, *The Living Theatre* (Avon: New York, 1972). Useful as a sourcebook with production breakdowns and an insight into Beck and Malina's working process.

Peter Brook, *The Empty Space* (Penguin: London, 1990). Brook's theatre manifesto.

Mladen Materic, *Organic Sequences in the Theatre* (Arts Documentation Unit: Exeter University, 1997). Video recording of Materic's workshop techniques.

Friedrich Nietzsche, *A Nietzsche Reader* (Penguin: London, 1977). Key texts by Nietzsche translated and selected by R.J. Hollingdale.

Anaïs Nin, *The Journals of Anaïs Nin: Vol. One* (Peter Owen: London, 1970), translated by Gunther Stuhlmann. A firsthand account of a friendship with Artaud.

Robert Pasolli, *A Book on the Open Theatre* (Avon: New York, 1970). An invaluable sourcebook of Chaikin's exercises and rehearsal processes.

Alan Read, *Theatre and Everyday Life: An Ethics of Performance* (Routledge: London, 2004).

Richard Schechner, *Public Domain: Essays on the Theatre* (The Bobbs-Merrill Company: New York). Schechner is a leading force in both practice and theory. For a more practical account of his work, I suggest *Environmental Theatre* (Applause: New York, 1994).

William H. Shephard, *The Dionysus Group* (Peter Lang: New York, 1991). A firsthand account of Schechner's working practice from an actor's perspective.

David Williams (ed.), *Peter Brook: A Theatrical Casebook* (Methuen: London, 1988). Contains a selection of reviews, interviews and articles surrounding *The Theatre of Cruelty Season* and *Marat-Sade* (amongst others). Of particular note is a reprint of Charles Marowitz's 'Notes on the Theatre of Cruelty' which details the rehearsal exercises used in 1964 at the RSC.

GREENWICH EXCHANGE BOOKS

STUDENT GUIDE LITERARY SERIES

The Greenwich Exchange Student Guide Literary Series is a collection of critical essays of major or contemporary serious writers in English and selected European languages. The series is for the student, the teacher and 'common readers' and is an ideal resource for libraries. The *Times Educational Supplement* praised these books, saying, "The style of [this series] has a pressure of meaning behind it. Readers should learn from that … If art is about selection, perception and taste, then this is it."

(ISBN prefix 978-1-871551- applies)
All books are paperbacks unless otherwise stated

The series includes:
W.H. Auden by Stephen Wade (36-5)
Honoré de Balzac by Wendy Mercer (48-8)
William Blake by Peter Davies (27-3)
The Brontës by Peter Davies (24-2)
Robert Browning by John Lucas (59-4)
Lord Byron by Andrew Keanie (83-9)
Samuel Taylor Coleridge by Andrew Keanie (64-8)
Joseph Conrad by Martin Seymour-Smith (18-1)
William Cowper by Michael Thorn (25-9)
Charles Dickens by Robert Giddings (26-9)
Emily Dickinson by Marnie Pomeroy (68-6)
John Donne by Sean Haldane (23-5)
Ford Madox Ford by Anthony Fowles (63-1)
The Stagecraft of Brian Friel by David Grant (74-7)
Robert Frost by Warren Hope (70-9)
Thomas Hardy by Sean Haldane (33-4)
Seamus Heaney by Warren Hope (37-2)
Joseph Heller by Anthony Fowles (84-6)
Gerard Manley Hopkins by Sean Sheehan (77-3)
James Joyce by Michael Murphy (73-0)
Philip Larkin by Warren Hope (35-8)
Laughter in the Dark – The Plays of Joe Orton by Arthur Burke (56-3)
Sylvia Plath by Marnie Pomeroy (88-4)
Poets of the First World War by John Greening (79-2)
Philip Roth by Paul McDonald (72-3)

Shakespeare's *A Midsummer Night's Dream* by Matt Simpson (90-7)
Shakespeare's *King Lear* by Peter Davies (95-2)
Shakespeare's *Macbeth* by Matt Simpson (69-3)
Shakespeare's *Othello* by Matt Simpson (71-6)
Shakespeare's Second Tetralogy: *Richard II – Henry V* by John Lucas (97-6)
Shakespeare's *The Merchant of Venice* by Alan Ablewhite (96-9)
Shakespeare's *The Tempest* by Matt Simpson (75-4)
Shakespeare's *Twelfth Night* by Matt Simpson (86-0)
Shakespeare's *The Winter's Tale* by John Lucas (80-3)
Shakespeare's Non-Dramatic Poetry by Martin Seymour-Smith (22-6)
Shakespeare's Sonnets by Martin Seymour-Smith (38-9)
Tobias Smollett by Robert Giddings (21-1)
Dylan Thomas by Peter Davies (78-5)
Alfred, Lord Tennyson by Michael Thorn (20-4)
William Wordsworth by Andrew Keanie (57-0)
W.B. Yeats by John Greening (34-1)

LITERATURE & BIOGRAPHY

Matthew Arnold and 'Thyrsis' *by Patrick Carill Connolly*
Matthew Arnold (1822-1888) was a leading poet, intellect and aesthete of the Victorian epoch. He is now best known for his strictures as a literary and cultural critic, and educationist. After a long period of neglect, his views have come in for a re-evaluation. Arnold's poetry remains less well known, yet his poems and his understanding of poetry, which defied the conventions of his time, were central to his achievement.

The author traces Arnold's intellectual and poetic development, showing how his poetry gathers its meanings from a lifetime's study of European literature and philosophy. Connolly's unique exegesis of 'Thyrsis' draws upon a wide-ranging analysis of the pastoral and its associated myths in both classical and native cultures. This study shows lucidly and in detail how Arnold encouraged the intense reflection of the mind on the subject placed before it, believing in " … the all importance of the choice of the subject, the necessity of accurate observation; and subordinate character of expression."

Patrick Carill Connolly gained his English degree at Reading University and taught English literature abroad for a number of years before returning to Britain. He is now a civil servant living in London.
2004 • 180 pages • ISBN 978-1-871551-61-7

The Author, the Book and the Reader *by Robert Giddings*
This collection of essays analyses the effects of changing technology and the attendant commercial pressures on literary styles and subject matter. Authors covered include Charles Dickens, Tobias Smollett, Mark Twain, Dr Johnson and John le Carré.
1991 • 220 pages • illustrated • ISBN 978-1-871551-01-3

Norman Cameron *by Warren Hope*
Cameron's poetry was admired by Auden; celebrated by Dylan Thomas; valued by Robert Graves. He was described by Martin Seymour-Smith as "one of ... the most rewarding and pure poets of his generation ..." and is at last given a full-length biography. This eminently sociable man, who had periods of darkness and despair, wrote little poetry by comparison with others of his time, but always a consistently high quality – imaginative and profound.
Warren Hope is a poet, a critic and university lecturer. He lives and works in Philadelphia, where he raised his family.
2000 • 226 pages • ISBN 978-1-871551-05-1

Aleister Crowley and the Cult of Pan *by Paul Newman*
Few more nightmarish figures stalk English literature than Aleister Crowley (1875-1947), poet, magician, mountaineer and agent provocateur. In this groundbreaking study, Paul Newman dives into the occult mire of Crowley's works and fishes out gems and grotesqueries that are by turns ethereal, sublime, pornographic and horrifying. Like Oscar Wilde before him, Crowley stood in "symbolic relationship to his age" and to contemporaries like Rupert Brooke, G.K. Chesterton and the Portuguese modernist, Fernando Pessoa. An influential exponent of the cult of the Great God Pan, his essentially 'pagan' outlook was shared by major European writers as well as English novelists like E.M. Forster, D.H. Lawrence and Arthur Machen.
Paul Newman lives in Cornwall. Editor of the literary magazine *Abraxas*, he has written over ten books.
2004 • 222 pages • ISBN 978-1-871551-66-2

John Dryden *by Anthony Fowles*
Of all the poets of the Augustan age, John Dryden was the most worldly. Anthony Fowles traces Dryden's evolution from 'wordsmith' to major poet. This critical study shows a poet of vigour and technical panache whose art was forged in the heat and battle of a turbulent polemical and pamphleteering age. Although Dryden's status as a literary critic has long been established,

Fowles draws attention to his neglected achievements as a translator of poetry. He deals also with the less well-known aspects of Dryden's work – his plays and occasional pieces.

Born in London and educated at the Universities of Oxford and Southern California, Anthony Fowles began his career in film-making before becoming an author of film and television scripts and more than twenty books. Readers will welcome the many contemporary references to novels and film with which Fowles illuminates the life and work of this decisively influential English poetic voice.

2003 • 292 pages • ISBN 978-1-871551-58-7

The Good That We Do *by John Lucas*
John Lucas' book blends fiction, biography and social history in order to tell the story of his grandfather, Horace Kelly. Headteacher of a succession of elementary schools in impoverished areas of London, 'Hod' Kelly was also a keen cricketer, a devotee of the music hall, and included among his friends the great trade union leader Ernest Bevin. In telling the story of his life, Lucas has provided a fascinating range of insights into the lives of ordinary Londoners from the First World War until the outbreak of the Second World War. Threaded throughout is an account of such people's hunger for education, and of the different ways government, church and educational officialdom ministered to that hunger. *The Good That We Do* is both a study of one man and of a period when England changed, drastically and forever.

John Lucas is Professor Emeritus of the Universities of Loughborough and Nottingham Trent. He is the author of numerous works of a critical and scholarly nature and has published eight collections of poetry.

2001 • 214 pages • ISBN 978-1-871551-54-9

D.H. Lawrence: The Nomadic Years, 1919-1930 *by Philip Callow*
This book provides a fresh insight into Lawrence's art as well as his life. Candid about the relationship between Lawrence and his wife, it shows nevertheless the strength of the bond between them. If no other book persuaded the reader of Lawrence's greatness, this does.

Philip Callow was born in Birmingham and studied engineering and teaching before he turned to writing. He has published 14 novels, several collections of short stories and poems, a volume of autobiography, and biographies on the lives of Chekhov, Cezanne, Robert Louis Stevenson, Walt Whitman and Van Gogh all of which have received critical acclaim. His biography of D.H. Lawrence's early years, *Son and Lover*, was widely praised.

2006 • 226 pages • ISBN 978-1-871551-82-2

Liar! Liar!: Jack Kerouac – Novelist *by R.J. Ellis*
The fullest study of Jack Kerouac's fiction to date. It is the first book to devote an individual chapter to every one of his novels. *On the Road*, *Visions of Cody* and *The Subterraneans* are reread in-depth, in a new and exciting way. *Visions of Gerard* and *Doctor Sax* are also strikingly reinterpreted, as are other daringly innovative writings, like 'The Railroad Earth' and his "try at a spontaneous *Finnegans Wake*" – *Old Angel Midnight*. Neglected writings, such as *Tristessa* and *Big Sur*, are also analysed, alongside better-known novels such as *Dharma Bums* and *Desolation Angels*.
R.J. Ellis is Senior Lecturer in English at Nottingham Trent University.
1999 • 294 pages • ISBN 978-1-871551-53-2

Musical Offering *by Yolanthe Leigh*
In a series of vivid sketches, anecdotes and reflections, Yolanthe Leigh tells the story of her growing up in the Poland of the 1930s and the Second World War. These are poignant episodes of a child's first encounters with both the enchantments and the cruelties of the world; and from a later time, stark memories of the brutality of the Nazi invasion, and the hardships of student life in Warsaw under the Occupation. But most of all this is a record of inward development; passages of remarkable intensity and simplicity describe the girl's response to religion, to music, and to her discovery of philosophy.
Yolanthe Leigh was formerly a Lecturer in Philosophy at Reading University.
2000 • 56 pages • ISBN: 978-1-871551-46-4

In Pursuit of Lewis Carroll *by Raphael Shaberman*
Sherlock Holmes and the author uncover new evidence in their investigations into the mysterious life and writing of Lewis Carroll. They examine published works by Carroll that have been overlooked by previous commentators. A newly-discovered poem, almost certainly by Carroll, is published here.
Amongst many aspects of Carroll's highly complex personality, this book explores his relationship with his parents, numerous child friends, and the formidable Mrs Liddell, mother of the immortal Alice. Raphael Shaberman was a founder member of the Lewis Carroll Society and a teacher of autistic children.
1994 • 118 pages • illustrated • ISBN 978-1-871551-13-6

Poetry in Exile: A study of the poetry of W.H. Auden, Joseph Brodsky & George Szirtes *by Michael Murphy*

"Michael Murphy discriminates the forms of exile and expatriation with the shrewdness of the cultural historian, the acuity of the literary critic, and the subtlety of a poet alert to the ways language and poetic form embody the precise contours of experience. His accounts of Auden, Brodsky and Szirtes not only cast much new light on the work of these complex and rewarding poets, but are themselves a pleasure to read." *Stan Smith, Research Professor in Literary Studies, Nottingham Trent University.*

Michael Murphy is a poet and critic. He teaches English literature at Liverpool Hope University College.

2004 • 266 pages • ISBN 978-1-871551-76-1

POETRY

Adam's Thoughts in Winter *by Warren Hope*

Warren Hope's poems have appeared from time to time in a number of literary periodicals, pamphlets and anthologies on both sides of the Atlantic. They appeal to lovers of poetry everywhere. His poems are brief, clear, frequently lyrical, characterised by wit, but often distinguished by tenderness. The poems gathered in this first book-length collection counter the brutalising ethos of contemporary life, speaking of, and for, the virtues of modesty, honesty and gentleness in an individual, memorable way.

2000 • 46 pages • ISBN 978-1-871551-40-2

Baudelaire: Les Fleurs du Mal *Translated by F.W. Leakey*

Selected poems from *Les Fleurs du Mal* are translated with parallel French texts and are designed to be read with pleasure by readers who have no French as well as those who are practised in the French language.

F.W. Leakey was Professor of French in the University of London. As a scholar, critic and teacher he specialised in the work of Baudelaire for 50 years and published a number of books on the poet.

2001 • 152 pages • ISBN 978-1-871551-10-5

'The Last Blackbird' and other poems by Ralph Hodgson *edited and introduced by John Harding*

Ralph Hodgson (1871-1962) was a poet and illustrator whose most influential and enduring work appeared to great acclaim just prior to, and during, the First World War. His work is imbued with a spiritual passion for the beauty of creation and the mystery of existence. This new selection brings together, for the first time in 40 years, some of the most beautiful and powerful 'hymns to life' in the English language.

John Harding lives in London. He is a freelance writer and teacher and is Ralph Hodgson's biographer.

2004 • 70 pages • ISBN 978-871551-81-5

Lines from the Stone Age *by Sean Haldane*
Reviewing Sean Haldane's 1992 volume *Desire in Belfast*, Robert Nye wrote in *The Times* that "Haldane can be sure of his place among the English poets." This place is not yet a conspicuous one, mainly because his early volumes appeared in Canada, and because he has earned his living by other means than literature. Despite this, his poems have always had their circle of readers. The 60 previously unpublished poems of *Lines from the Stone Age* – "lines of longing, terror, pride, lust and pain" – may widen this circle.

2000 • 52 pages • ISBN 978-1-871551-39-6

Lipstick *by Maggie Butt*
Lipstick is Maggie Butt's debut collection of poems and marks the entrance of a voice at once questioning and self-assured. She believes that poetry should be the tip of the stiletto which slips between the ribs directly into the heart. The poems of *Lipstick* are often deceptively simple, unafraid of focusing on such traditional themes as time, loss and love through a range of lenses and personae. Maggie Butt is capable of speaking in the voice of an 11th-century stonemason, a Himalayan villager, a 13-year-old anorexic. When writing of such everyday things as nylon sheets, jumble sales, X-rays or ginger beer, she brings to her subjects a dry humour and an acute insight. But beyond the intimate and domestic, her poems cover the world, from Mexico to Russia; they deal with war, with the resilience of women, and, most of all, with love.
Maggie Butt is head of Media and Communication at Middlesex University, London, where she has taught Creative Writing since 1990.

2007 • 72 pages • ISBN 978-1-871551-94-5

Martin Seymour-Smith – Collected Poems *edited by Peter Davies*
To the general public Martin Seymour-Smith (1928-1998) is known as a distinguished literary biographer, notably of Robert Graves, Rudyard Kipling and Thomas Hardy. To such figures as John Dover Wilson, William Empson, Stephen Spender and Anthony Burgess, he was regarded as one of the most independently-minded scholars of his generation, through his pioneering critical edition of Shakespeare's *Sonnets*, and his magisterial *Guide to Modern World Literature*.
To his fellow poets, Graves, James Reeves, C.H. Sisson and Robert Nye – he was first and foremost a poet. As this collection demonstrates, at the

centre of the poems is a passionate engagement with Man, his sexuality and his personal relationships.

2006 • 182 pages • ISBN 978-1-871551-47-1

Shakespeare's Sonnets *by Martin Seymour-Smith*
Martin Seymour-Smith's outstanding achievement lies in the field of literary biography and criticism. In 1963 he produced his comprehensive edition, in the old spelling, of *Shakespeare's Sonnets* (here revised and corrected by himself and Peter Davies in 1998). With its landmark introduction and its brilliant critical commentary on each sonnet, it was praised by William Empson and John Dover Wilson. Stephen Spender said of him "I greatly admire Martin Seymour-Smith for the independence of his views and the great interest of his mind"; and both Robert Graves and Anthony Burgess described him as the leading critic of his time. His exegesis of the *Sonnets* remains unsurpassed.

2001 • 194 pages • ISBN 978-1-871551-38-9

The Rain and the Glass *by Robert Nye*
When Robert Nye's first poems were published, G.S. Fraser declared in the *Times Literary Supplement*: "Here is a proper poet, though it is hard to see how the larger literary public (greedy for flattery of their own concerns) could be brought to recognize that. But other proper poets – how many of them are left? – will recognize one of themselves."
Since then Nye has become known to a large public for his novels, especially *Falstaff* (1976), winner of the Hawthornden Prize and The Guardian Fiction Prize, and *The Late Mr Shakespeare* (1998). But his true vocation has always been poetry, and it is as a poet that he is best known to his fellow poets.
This book contains all the poems Nye has written since his *Collected Poems* of 1995, together with his own selection from that volume. An introduction, telling the story of his poetic beginnings, affirms Nye's unfashionable belief in inspiration, as well as defining that quality of unforced truth which distinguishes the best of his work: "I have spent my life trying to write poems, but the poems gathered here came mostly when I was not."

2005 • 132 pages • ISBN 978-1-871551-41-9

Wilderness *by Martin Seymour-Smith*
This is Martin Seymour-Smith's first publication of his poetry for more than twenty years. This collection of 36 poems is a fearless account of an inner life of love, frustration, guilt, laughter and the celebration of others. He is best known to the general public as the author of the controversial and bestselling *Hardy* (1994).

1994 • 52 pages • ISBN 978-1-871551-08-2

EDUCATION

Making School Work *by Andy Buck*
Full of practical examples, this book sets out a range of strategies for successful school leadership. It provides examples of tried and tested ideas to use when tackling some of the key challenges facing every school leader: This book aims to offer readers a range of practical approaches to both policy and leadership style, based around a series of case studies and school-based policies. Each chapter examines a key challenge facing school leaders and provides practical ideas and strategies that have been shown to work in schools.

A geography teacher since 1987, Andy Bucks' experience has included working as a head of department, head of year, deputy head and two headships, all in London schools.

2007 • 142 pages • ISBN 978-1-871551-52-5

HISTORICAL FACTION

The Secret Life of Elizabeth I *by Paul Doherty*
A detective story with a difference – tracking down the real Elizabeth I – capturing the atmosphere of Elizabethan and Jacobean England, with stunning results. Paul Doherty's original research shows Elizabeth I of England to be a strongwilled, brilliant ruler but also a woman with deep passions and fervent attachments. The lady-in-waiting describes the passionate relationship between Elizabeth and Robert Dudley, later Earl of Leicester. She reveals evidence about the strange death of Dudley's wife, the very physical relationship between Elizabeth and Dudley, and the stunning revelation that they had a son, Arthur Dudley, seized by the Spanish in 1587.

Paul Doherty is an internationally renowned author. He studied history at Liverpool and Oxford Universities, gaining his doctorate at Oxford. He is now the headmaster of a very successful London school. First in the series published by Greenwich Exchange.

2006 • 210 pages • ISBN 978-1-871551-85-3 (Hardback)

Death of the Red King *by Paul Doherty*
Was William Rufus, the Red King, accidentally killed by one of his own men while hunting or is there a more chilling interpretation of his death? Doherty demonstrates that the Red King's death is highly suspect. Walter Tirel has been cast as the villain of the piece. However, through the eyes of Anselm the great philosopher, this faction develops a quite different version

of his death.
Second in the series published by Greenwich Exchange.
2006 • 190 pages • ISBN 978-1-871551-92-1 (Hardback)

BUSINESS

English Language Skills *by Vera Hughes*
If you want to be sure, (as a student, or in your business or personal life), that your written English is correct, this book is for you. Vera Hughes' aim is to help you to remember the basic rules of spelling, grammar and punctuation. 'Noun', 'verb', 'subject', 'object' and 'adjective' are the only technical terms used. The book teaches the clear, accurate English required by the business and office world. It coaches acceptable current usage and makes the rules easier to remember.

Vera Hughes was a civil servant and is a trainer and author of training manuals.
2002 • 142 pages • ISBN 978-1-871551-60-0